Bob Warden's

SLOW FOOD FAST

Over 120 Quick and Hearty

Pressure Cooker Recipes

Bob Warden

Published By Dynamic Housewares Inc

First paperback edition 2009

For information about special discounts for bulk purchases
please contact sales@dynamichousewares.com

Please read and adhere to all manufacturer's manuals
before operating any kitchen device.

Author: Robert Warden with Christian Stella

Manufactured in the USA

ISBN 978-0-9841887-1-0

TABLE OF CONTENTS

Introduction

The Modern Pressure Cooker

My FASCINATION WITH PRESSURE cookers began at a young age, watching my mother wield several of the old fashioned variety at the same time. She was constantly regulating the heat on the stove to keep each at its appropriate temperature.

She had it mastered. Thanksgivings were particularly showy, all cookers blazing while I stood in awe and the rest of the family stared like they were witnessing a woman on the edge.

Watching my mother in the kitchen on our farm in Iowa, I would have never guessed that one day I'd be equipping my own mass of pressure cookers in front of television cameras. Demonstrating something I'm truly passionate about. Moving from cooker to cooker, releasing the pressure on one and then the next. Cooking an entire feast all at once, just as my mother did so many years ago. But let's not sell her short.

Today's electronic cookers do all the work for you. They generate their own heat to minimize the scorching of a high heat stovetop, they heat to the appropriate temperature to build the exact amount of pressure at the touch of a button and they have multiple safety features in place to keep the pressure in the cooker and not all over your kitchen's ceiling.

I've written this book to share the favorite of my pressure cooker recipes. Recipes from the farm in Iowa while I was growing up, recipes I developed on air at QVC and all the recipes in between. Like pressure cookers themselves, things have changed over the years. Ingredients are easier to come by than ever, available in more convenient forms that require less grunt work. By far, these are the fastest recipes for the heartiest family style dishes that I've ever compiled.

Most of all, I'd like to show that a pressure cooker is a truly versatile tool, capable of cooking more than just a pot roast. My mother knew it all those years ago with all those cookers on the stove. Then again, she did cook a darn good pot roast.

Electronic

Pressure Cookers

THE RECIPES IN THIS BOOK WERE specifically written and tested on an electronic pressure cooker. If you own a stovetop, non-electric pressure cooker, turn to the next page for tips on making the recipes in this book.

Please refer to the instruction manual that came with your pressure cooker, reading and adhering to all warnings and precautions before attempting to make any recipes in this book! As there are many varieties of pressure cookers on the market, your manual should be your final source of guidance in using your particular make of pressure cooker.

Electronic pressure cookers are an all in one solution to pressure cooking that are extremely safe, energy efficient and easy to operate. Much like a modern crock-pot or slow cooker (in fact many pressure cookers also include a slow cooker setting), electronic pressure cookers generate their own cooking heat and do all of the cooking for you, based on internal gauges and the settings that you input on the digital display.

Most cookers have two heat settings, high and low and the recipes in this book are written with that in mind. Your cooker may also have a medium setting, which you can disregard when following my recipes.

Some electronic pressure cookers forego the high and low cook settings and display the amount of cooking pressure using the term "PSI" or pounds per square inch. For these cookers, the recipes in this book that are listed to be cooked on "high" can be cooked at 12-15psi and the recipes to be cooked on "low" can be cooked at 5-8psi.

Other electronic pressure cookers use the term "kPa" to display cooking power. For these cookers, consider "high" to be 80kPa and "low" to be 40kPa.

The recipes in this book refer to two methods for releasing the pressure after cooking. A "quick release" involves releasing the pressure rapidly via your model of cooker's pressure release valve to stop the cooking. A "natural release" is when you simply let the cooker sit after cooking until the built up pressure dissipates on its own. For more on how to safely perform these specific actions, refer to the manual that came with your particular model.

Stovetop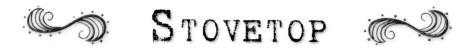
Pressure Cookers

T HOUGH THE RECIPES IN THIS BOOK were specifically written for an electronic pressure cooker, if you own a stovetop, traditional pressure cooker, they can be made quite easily and with very little adaptation.

Please refer to the instruction manual that came with your pressure cooker, reading and adhering to all warnings and precautions before attempting to make any recipes in this book! As there are many varieties of pressure cookers on the market, your manual should be your final source of guidance in using your particular make of pressure cooker.

The recipes in this book use the terms "high" and "low" as cooking temperatures, standard settings for an electronic cooker. Stovetop pressure cookers almost always calculate the temperature in "PSI" or pounds per square inch. For these stovetop cookers, the recipes in this book that are listed to be cooked on "high" can be cooked at 15psi and the recipes to be cooked on "low" can be cooked at 7 1/2psi.

Once you've brought your stovetop cooker up to the proper psi, immediately lower the stove's heat to medium or as low as you need for your cooker to maintain that constant psi.

The recipes in this book refer to two methods for releasing the pressure after cooking. A "quick release" involves releasing the pressure rapidly via your

model of cooker's pressure release valve to stop the cooking. A "natural release" is when you simply let the cooker sit after cooking until the built up pressure dissipates on its own. Some stovetop cookers require you to run cold water over the lid to rapidly release the pressure and perform what this book refers to as a "quick release". For more on how to safely perform these specific actions, refer to the manual that came with your particular model.

As many stovetop cookers are exposed to a harsher heat source (your stove) than the ones built into an electronic cooker, it is recommended that you place a heat diffuser between the stove and the cooker when cooking beans, rice, pasta or desserts to reduce food sticking and possibly burning.

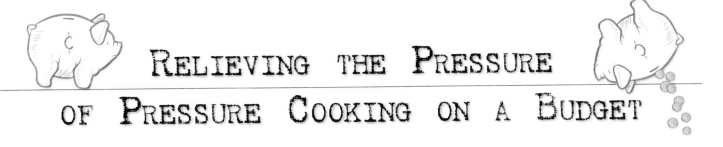

Relieving the Pressure of Pressure Cooking on a Budget

When it comes to what you eat, saving money doesn't mean you have to sacrifice quality. I'm a firm believer that the ingredients make the dish, but that doesn't mean I'm not thrifty! I am always looking for a better way, whether I'm tinkering with a new recipe or in the case of saving money… grocery shopping. Now with prices increasing and food products shrinking, here are a few ways I've found to let the air out of a ballooning grocery bill.

Buy in bulk. Pressure cooking is perfect for bulk shopping. When you can cook an entire roast in under an hour, there's no reason to wait for special occasions to make one up. Not only are roasts usually cheaper than smaller cuts of meat, they're all but guaranteed to yield lunch money saving leftovers!

Shop the ads. I'll usually choose which recipes to cook for the week based on whether or not the ingredients are on sale. While most people look to sales on meats to make up their minds, I like to make recipes with at least two or three of the ingredients on sale. With over 120 in this book, it's not as hard as it sounds!

Start an herb garden. Fresh herbs are very low maintenance plants and you'll probably find that once they start growing, they just don't stop! A few packets of seeds for only a few dollars and you'll be in the green. When they're growing too fast to use up, try drying them in a food dehydrator and giving jars of the freshest dried herbs you've ever had as gifts.

Buy inexpensive cuts of meat. I use my pressure cooker almost every day, but you'd never see me cooking a filet mignon in it! It's unnecessary, as inexpensive and ordinarily tough cuts of meat like round steak can cook to fork tender in minutes.

Keep a well stocked pantry. While it may seem expensive to overstock a pantry, it really does pay off over time. Last minute meals and snacks will be readily prepared, saving you from ordering out. Dried beans are a great source of protein when you don't have any meat in the fridge and the pressure cooker can cook them up in no time.

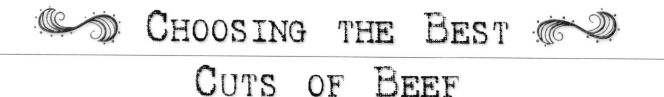

Choosing the Best Cuts of Beef

With all of the pressure cooking that I do, sometimes I feel like the grocery store is my second home! A good grocery store with a great meat case is a thing of beauty, beckoning you to cook to your heart's content. That is, as long as you have an idea of what you're looking for.

While pressure cooking is an exciting, energy efficient, fast and flavorful way to cook—it doesn't change one of the main fundamentals of cooking—to make good food, you're going to need good ingredients. What it may change, however, is your perception of just what is good.

When shopping for beef, typically the most inexpensive cuts are also the toughest. With tons of connecting tissue for your teeth to chew and very little fat marbled throughout them, they're certainly not butter knife tender and have nothing to keep them moist. Round, chuck and brisket roasts or steaks all fall into this category. Round steaks (pictured) look beautiful until you grill, broil or skillet fry them, take a bite and realize that your creation is as tough as shoe leather. But

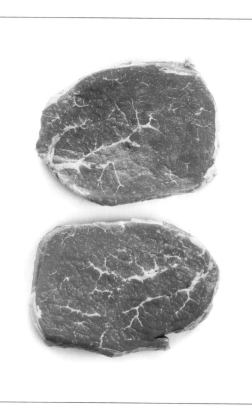

these are good, healthier cuts of meat with less fat and even more of a concentrated beef flavor than the more expensive, "tender" cuts of beef.

Typically, slow cooking tough cuts of beef for several hours is the best option, especially with roasts. This is where the pressure cooker really shines, producing the same, tender results in under an hour. Now, inexpensive roasts and tough cuts of meat literally fall apart in a realistic amount of time.

Keep in mind that chuck and round roasts are interchangeable, with the same cooking time for any recipe you use them in. This is good to know when one goes on sale or simply is not available. Though the pressure cooker does a great job of breaking up the tough connecting tissue of just about any cut of meat, chuck roasts have more fat than round and will cook to be even more tender. It's up to you whether you prefer slightly more tender or slightly less fat. With all cuts of meat, I would highly suggest finding the most uniformly thick piece, for nice and even cooking.

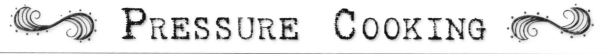

PRESSURE COOKING
PRODUCE

THOUGH A PRESSURE COOKER CAN DO a number on even the toughest cuts of meat, it is still a highly versatile piece of equipment entirely capable of cooking fresh and perfectly cooked fruits and vegetables.

The secrets to pressure cooked vegetables that aren't overcooked are lightning fast cooking times followed by a quick release of the pressure. In the case of more delicate vegetables, such as broccoli florets, the margin between perfectly cooked and completely overdone is as thin as 1 minute.

The firmer the vegetable, the better results you will have. Squash, with their thick rind cook particularly well and you may find that the pressure cooker can make the best corn on the cob you've ever had in no time at all.

A metal steamer basket, small enough to fit into the pressure cooker, will yield better results as it lifts the vegetables out of the liquid necessary to cook. Many companies sell them specifically for pressure cookers and they're mostly interchangeable regardless of brand, as long as they're made for the same quart cooker. The easiest place to find them is online, but an in-store fix can be had by purchasing a small metal colander instead.

Cooking a one pot meal with meat and vegetables will almost always benefit from a two step cooking process. Refer to my cooking charts to find the cook time of your longest cooking vegetable and then stop the cooking process short by that much time, releasing the pressure with a quick release. Then, add the vegetables and cook for their recommended time. Release the pressure with a second quick release for the a perfectly cooked one pot meal. While it may seem inconvenient, you can chop and prep the vegetables during the first step of cooking to save time!

Speaking of saving time, when you first remove the lid on a finished dish it is often so hot that a bag of frozen vegetables can be stirred right in and completely cooked through residual heat. Take the bag out of the freezer and leave on the counter as the dish is cooking to slightly thaw by the time the pressure cooker's lid comes off.

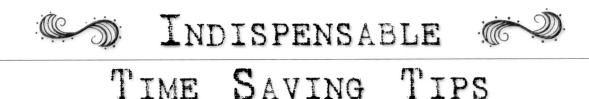

Indispensable
Time Saving Tips

Time is of the essence! Whether you're always on the go or a hungry family is always at your heels, pressure cooking is here to save the minutes of the day. The following time saving tips can save you even more of those minutes; while it may seem that they're getting into the minutiae of cooking, for me, every second counts!

Arrange and prep your ingredients first. Grab all of your pantry items and spices before you start cooking to minimize back and forth trips. Measure and cut your ingredients at the same time and following the cooking steps of a recipe will be as easy as 1 2 3.

Plan accordingly. Plan the entire meal and how you will prepare it in advance to utilize multiple cooking methods. Plan to make a salad while dinner is in the pressure cooker or plan to have a pot of water heating on the stove for pasta as you prep the meat course ingredients for the pressure cooker. This way, everything will come out at the same time.

Cook a one pot meal. It should go without saying that the pressure cooker makes perfect one pot meals, saving tons of time on cleanup.

Cut meat into smaller portions. Cutting a roast into 2 inch thick pieces to cook under pressure can cut your cooking time in half.

Chop extra. If a recipe calls for half of a diced onion, dice the whole thing and save the excess in a food storage bag or container in the fridge for use later in the week. Chopped onion is always good to have on hand. It freezes well too, so why not chop a few?

Use frozen vegetables. With the pressure cooker, the cooking time of vegetables is not exactly an issue, but the cleaning and chopping time just may be. Cut time by letting the frozen food aisle cut things for you! Most stores also sell chopped fresh vegetables in the produce aisle now and jarred minced garlic will have you asking who spends their time peeling garlic these days?

Use your pressure cooker's quick release valve! What are you waiting for? Letting the pressure release naturally is not always necessary.

PANTRY
SHOPPING LIST

Being prepared from the start can save you a ton of time, both at home and in the grocery store. The following lists include the ingredients used most throughout the recipes in this book. I would suggest filling the gaps in your spice cabinet first.

SPICES

bay leaves

cayenne pepper

celery salt

chili powder

cinnamon

cumin

garlic powder

Italian seasoning

mustard powder

nutmeg

onion powder

oregano

paprika

parsley flakes

poultry seasoning

rosemary

tarragon

thyme

white pepper

DRY GOODS

beef base

chicken base

cooked bacon pieces

diced tomatoes, canned

Dijon mustard

flour

ketchup

lemon juice

light brown sugar

minced garlic

olive oil

red wine

sugar

tomato paste

vanilla extract

vegetable broth

vegetable oil

vinegar

white wine

worcestershire sauce

yellow mustard

PERISHABLES

bell peppers

butter

carrots

celery

cream cheese

eggs

lemons

milk

onions

Parmesan cheese

redskin potatoes

sour cream

STOCKING UP ON BASES

BIG FLAVOR IN A SMALL PACKAGE

ALL FOODS COOKED IN A PRESSURE cooker require at least 1/2 cup of liquid to create the steam necessary to bring the cooker up to pressure. In most cases, pressure cooking in water would be a waste of a layer of flavor that you can add to the final dish. When it comes to good cooking in general, layering flavors is key. That's where a good stock or broth comes in.

Making fresh stocks is a time consuming process that few people actually undertake and cans or cartons of chicken, beef, vegetable and other stocks or broths are extremely lacking in the flavor department. Bouillon cubes are so salty that the only thing I'd do with them is paint numbers on them and play Yahtzee. So what is there to use?

Bases. Bases are a high quality, highly concentrated paste that dissolves into a broth when added to water. The small five inch tall jars are available in a wide variety of flavors, near the canned broths in just about any grocery store. The most readily available brand is called *Better than Bouillon*. While the jars usually cost around five dollars each, they make almost 40 cups of broth, which would cost

over twenty dollars canned. Quite simply, bases are the cheapest and lightest way to carry home 10 quarts of a good quality broth.

Bases come in all sorts of flavors, from chicken and beef, to vegetable, mushroom and even ham! While writing this book, I visited a dozen grocery stores and they all carried chicken and beef base, but only two carried the full gamut of flavors. For this reason, I have only included chicken and beef in this book. I highly recommend picking up a jar of vegetable base if you see it and substituting it (mixed with water) for the vegetable broth listed in my recipes.

Bases are not only made from real chicken, beef or vegetables, they are the perfect choice for preparing recipes because you only make what you need.

Most **bases are turned into broth by mixing 1 teaspoon with 1 cup of water**, though they allow the flexibility of adjusting that amount to your taste. I like to add a small amount extra when cooking with a lot of water releasing vegetables such as onions or mushrooms.

The jars must be refrigerated after opening but last for up to a year.

SOUPS

Minestrone Soup with Tortellini	15
Ground Beef Chili	16
Chicken and Sausage Gumbo	17
Cabbage Soup with Polish Sausage	19
Butternut Squash Soup	20
Southern Seafood Gumbo	21
Cooled Cucumber and Coconut Soup	23
Spinach and Lentil Soup	24
Crab and Corn Bisque	25
Cinnamon Spiced Turkey Chili	27
Black Bean Soup	29
Split Pea and Bacon Soup	30
Brunswick Stew	31
Cream of Chicken Soup with Gnocchi Dumplings	33

Prep Time	Cook Time	Serves	Temperature
15 MINS	5 MINS	SIX	HIGH

MINESTRONE SOUP WITH TORTELLINI

SOUPS

Loosely translated from Italian, Minestrone means "The Big Soup" for a reason. Though its ingredients have never been set in stone, one thing has; it's fit to be a full meal. This take is certainly no different with spoon after spoon of plump cheese stuffed tortellini; your family won't believe it went from fridge to table in only 20 minutes.

1. ADD the oil to the pressure cooker and heat on high or "brown" with the lid off. Sauté onions, celery, carrots and garlic until onions begin to sweat.

2. ADD the remaining ingredients and stir. Securely lock on the pressure cooker's lid, set the cooker to high and cook for 5 minutes.

3. PERFORM a quick release to release the cooker's pressure. Safely remove lid and check tortellini for doneness. If it is too al dente for your likeness continue to boil on high or "brown" with the lid off until it is where you want it. Serve topped with shredded or freshly grated Parmesan cheese.

SHOPPING LIST

2 tablespoons **olive oil**

1 **white onion**, chopped small

2 stalks **celery**, cut into 1/4 inch slices

2 **carrots**, sliced into 1/4 inch discs

1 tablespoon **minced garlic**

8 ounces package **cheese tortellini** (available in the regular, dry goods pasta aisle)

4 cups **vegetable broth**

1 jar **spaghetti sauce**

1 can **diced tomatoes**

1 1/2 teaspoons **Italian seasoning**

1 teaspoon **sugar**

1/4 teaspoon **ground black pepper**

shredded Parmesan cheese, for garnish

Bob's Tips

These days there are plenty of varieties of jarred spaghetti sauces and dried tortellini to choose from, so why not try making this recipe with a jar of chunky mushroom tomato sauce or spinach tortellini or both?

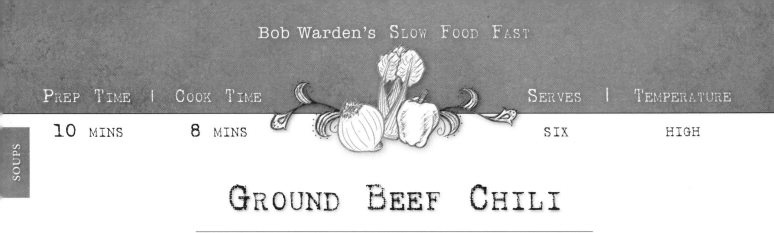

Prep Time	Cook Time		Serves	Temperature
10 MINS	8 MINS		SIX	HIGH

GROUND BEEF CHILI

SOUPS

Make sure you have plenty of crackers on hand when preparing this wintertime classic. My legume free recipe is a terrific base to add a can or two of whichever beans you have in the pantry.

1. Add the vegetable oil to the pressure cooker and heat on high or "brown" with the lid off until sizzling. Add the ground beef, breaking it up with spoon or spatula as it browns.

2. Once the ground beef is browning well, add the chopped onion and minced garlic and stir in for 2 minutes.

3. Add the remaining ingredients, except for cheddar cheese and stir. Securely lock on the pressure cooker's lid, set the cooker to high and cook for 8 minutes.

4. Let the pressure release naturally for 10 minutes before quick releasing the remaining pressure and safely removing lid. Salt and pepper to taste and serve topped with shredded cheddar cheese.

SHOPPING LIST

1 tablespoon **vegetable oil**

2 pounds **lean ground beef**

1 cup **onion**, chopped large

1 tablespoon **minced garlic**

1 can **diced tomatoes**, with liquid (14-16 ounces)

2 teaspoons **chicken base** (see page: 12) mixed into 2 cups water

1 can **mild green chile peppers**, with liquid (4 ounces)

1 teaspoon **sugar**

1/2 teaspoon **cumin**

2 teaspoons **chili powder**

2 tablespoons **cornmeal**

salt and pepper to taste

shredded cheddar cheese, for garnish

Bob's Tips

Chili is a prime dish for all sorts of wonderful toppings. Shredded cheddar cheese goes without saying, but how about spicy pepper jack cheese? Sour cream, plain yogurt or even avocado can cool things down a bit. Chopped onions or even green onion tops can add a little flavor and crunch.

Prep Time	Cook Time			Serves	Temperature
15 MINS	6 MINS			SIX	HIGH

CHICKEN AND SAUSAGE GUMBO

Soups

WHILE TYPICALLY SERVED OVER RICE, this one pot Louisiana gumbo is cooked all at once in only 6 minutes! This hearty, Creole stew gets its name, Gumbo, from an African word for okra and for good reason; as okra is pulling double duty here by actually thickening the soup as it cooks!

1. ADD the butter, garlic, sausage, onion, bell pepper and celery to pressure cooker and cook on high or "brown" with lid off until sausage begins to brown and vegetables begin to sweat.

2. COAT chicken thigh slices with the flour on all sides before adding them to the cooker.

3. ADD the remaining ingredients and stir. Securely lock on the pressure cooker's lid, set the cooker to high and cook for 6 minutes.

4. LET the pressure release naturally for 10 minutes before quick releasing the remaining pressure and safely removing the lid. Salt and pepper to taste before serving.

SHOPPING LIST

2 tablespoons **butter**

1 tablespoon **minced garlic**

1/2 pound **andouille or smoked sausage**, cut into 1/4 inch slices

1 cup **onion**, chopped large

1 **green bell pepper**, chopped large

2 **stalks celery**, cut into 1/4 inch slices

1 pound **boneless, skinless chicken thighs**, each thigh cut into 3 strips

3 tablespoons **flour**

1 1/2 cups **frozen okra slices**

1 cup **white rice**, uncooked

4 teaspoons **chicken base** (see page: 12) mixed into 4 cups water

1 can **diced tomatoes** (14-16 ounces)

2 **bay leaves**

1 tablespoon **parsley flakes**

1 teaspoon **onion powder**

1/2 teaspoon **paprika**

1/2 teaspoon **ground red or cayenne pepper**

salt and pepper to taste

If you aren't a fan of spicy foods, you may want to omit the ground red pepper in this dish and if you are a fan of spicy foods, you'll definitely want to bring a bottle of Louisiana hot sauce or Tobasco to the table with it.

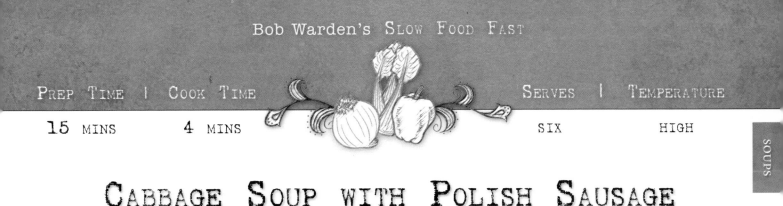

Prep Time	Cook Time		Serves	Temperature
15 MINS	4 MINS		SIX	HIGH

CABBAGE SOUP WITH POLISH SAUSAGE

SOUPS

IF IT'S POSSIBLE FOR A SOUP TO BE BOTH hearty and light at the same time, this is the one. The combination of the chunky potatoes, sausage and loads of cabbage with such a light and refreshing broth is a sure fire success for any dinner with guests!

1. ADD the butter to the pressure cooker and heat on high or "brown" with the lid off. Sauté onions and minced garlic in butter until onions begin to brown.

2. ADD the remaining ingredients and stir. Securely lock on the pressure cooker's lid, set the cooker to high and cook for 4 minutes.

3. PERFORM a quick release to release the cooker's pressure. Safely remove lid and serve.

SHOPPING LIST

2 tablespoons **butter or margarine**

1 white **onion**, sliced into 1/6 inch rings

1 1/2 teaspoons **minced garlic**

4 cups sliced **cabbage** (may use coleslaw shreds, sold in bagged lettuce section)

2 cups **red potatoes**, cut in 1/2 inch cubes with skin on

8 ounces **smoked kielbasa sausage**, sliced into thick discs, then cubed

2 teaspoons **chicken base** (see page: 12) mixed into 2 cups water

2 cups **vegetable broth**

1 tablespoon **white vinegar**

1 tablespoon **dried parsley**

1 **bay leaf**

1 teaspoon **celery salt**

1 teaspoon **sugar**

1/4 teaspoon **ground black pepper**

This soup goes great with a nice rye bread. For a creamier broth, mix 1/4 cup of half and half into the pot just before serving, or try garnishing with a dollop of sour cream.

SOUPS

Prep Time	Cook Time	Serves	Temperature
10 MINS	8 MINS	SIX	HIGH

Butternut Squash Soup

Soups

THIS TASTY SOUP HAS BECOME A Thanksgiving staple for my family. We get a big pot started first thing in the morning and use it to not only kick start the wonderful smells in the house but to stave off appetites that can't quite wait until the big meal.

1. HEAT olive oil, garlic and onion in pressure cooker on high or "brown" with lid off until onions are sizzling and begin to sweat.

2. COVER with remaining ingredients, except for half and half. Securely lock on the pressure cooker's lid, set the cooker to high and cook for 8 minutes.

SHOPPING LIST

1 tablespoon **olive oil**

2 teaspoons **minced garlic**

1/2 **onion**, diced

2 medium sized **butternut squash**, peeled and seeded and cut into 2 inch chunks

3 teaspoons **chicken base** (see page: 12) mixed into 3 cups water

1/2 teaspoon **ground sage**

1/8 teaspoon **nutmeg**

1/4 cup **half and half**

salt and pepper to taste

3. PERFORM a quick release to release the cooker's pressure. Safely remove lid and using a slotted spoon, transfer butternut squash chunks to a food processor or blender. Add half and half and blend until smooth.

4. REINTRODUCE blended squash and half and half to the cooking pot, mixing with cooking liquid until combined well. Serve hot. If soup has cooled, heat on high or "brown" with lid off until hot.

If squash is too thick to blend smoothly, add a ladle or two of the cooking liquid until there is enough liquid to blend. Try serving with a dollop of plain yogurt to make the soup even creamier.

Prep Time	Cook Time		Serves	Temperature
15 MINS	3 MINS		SIX	HIGH

SOUPS

SOUTHERN SEAFOOD GUMBO

SOUPS

A GOOD SEAFOOD GUMBO IS LIKE A WHO'S Who of everything delicious in the ocean. Serve it in large bowls, leaving plenty of room to stir in some white rice. Make up some hush puppies to go with it and you are one spoonful away from utter contentment.

1. ADD all ingredients to pressure cooker and stir. Securely lock on the pressure cooker's lid, set the cooker to high and cook for 3 minutes.

2. PERFORM a quick release to release the cooker's pressure and safely remove lid. Salt and pepper to taste before serving as is or over rice.

SHOPPING LIST

1 pound **white fish filets** (cod, haddock, etc.) cut into 1 inch pieces

1 pound **shrimp**, peeled and deveined

1/2 pound **lump crabmeat**, optional

2 tablespoons **butter or margarine**

1 tablespoon **minced garlic**

1 **onion**, chopped

1 **red bell pepper**, chopped

2 stalks **celery**, cut into 1/4 inch slices

1 1/2 cups **frozen, sliced okra**

3 teaspoons **chicken base** (see page: 12) mixed into 3 cups water

1 can **diced tomatoes** (14-16 ounces)

2 **bay leaves**

1 teaspoon **onion powder**

1 tablespoon **Old Bay seasoning**

1/2 teaspoon **ground red or cayenne pepper**

salt and pepper to taste

Bob's Tips

If the gumbo is too thin for your taste you can thicken it with two tablespoons of corn starch mixed into two tablespoons water. Set the cooker to high or "brown" with the lid off and stir in corn starch while simmering, until thickened.

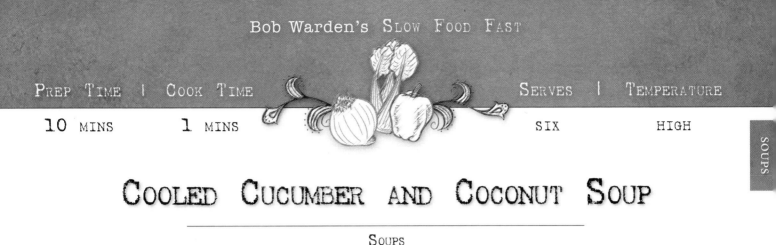

Prep Time	Cook Time	Serves	Temperature
10 MINS	1 MINS	SIX	HIGH

SOUPS

Cooled Cucumber and Coconut Soup

Soups

A COLD SOUP MAY BE THE LAST THING you'd expect to cook in a pressure cooker, but you've got to give it a try! This soup could technically be made without cooking at all, but cooking it for 1 minutes under pressure brings out all sorts of wonderful flavors and then locks them in for a refreshing dish on a hot summer day.

1. RESERVE 1 cucumber for garnish. Peel 2 cucumbers, and then slice in half lengthwise. Spoon out the softer, seed filled portion in the center and discard. Roughly chop the peeled and cleaned cucumber halves.

2. HEAT olive oil, garlic and onion in pressure cooker on high or "brown" with lid off until onions are sizzling and begin to sweat.

SHOPPING LIST

3 medium sized **cucumbers**

1 tablespoon **olive oil**

1 teaspoon **minced garlic**

1/2 **onion**, diced

1 cup **vegetable broth**

1 tablespoon **lime juice**

1/2 teaspoon **salt**

1/4 teaspoon **ground black pepper**

2 teaspoons **sugar**

1 can **unsweetened coconut milk** (14-16 ounces)

shredded coconut, toasted, for garnish

3. COVER with remaining ingredients, except for coconut milk and toasted coconut. Securely lock on the pressure cooker's lid, set the cooker to high and cook for 1 minute.

4. PERFORM a quick release to release the cooker's pressure. Safely remove lid and stir in coconut milk. Cover and refrigerate for 2 hours until cold.

5. BLEND cold soup in a blender or food processor until smooth. Serve topped with thinly sliced cucumber and toasted coconut.

To toast shredded coconut: preheat an oven to 350 degrees and spread coconut on a sheet pan in a thin layer. Bake 6-8 minutes, shaking sheet pan halfway through to stir around.

Prep Time	Cook Time	Serves	Temperature
10 MINS	8 MINS	SIX	HIGH

SOUPS

SPINACH AND LENTIL SOUP

SOUPS

THIS REFRESHING SOUP'S LIGHT FLAVORS are delicious but not overpowering. One of the great things about pressure cooking is that it makes lentils an everyday ingredient, no longer too time consuming to prepare. Quite simply, they're one of the most balanced foods on the planet, loaded with protein, fiber and even iron!

1. RINSE lentils in a colander, picking through them to make sure there are no stones or other objects.

2. ADD all ingredients to pressure cooker, except spinach and stir. Securely lock on pressure cooker's lid, set the cooker to high and cook for 8 minutes.

3. PERFORM a quick release to release the cooker's pressure and safely remove lid. Stir in thawed spinach and salt and pepper to taste. Serve immediately.

SHOPPING LIST

1 cup **dried lentils**

2 stalks **celery**, chopped

2 **carrots**, peeled and chopped

2 tablespoons **olive oil**

1 tablespoon **minced garlic**

4 teaspoons **chicken base** (see page: 12) mixed into 4 cups water

2 cups **vegetable broth**

2 tablespoons **lemon juice**

1 teaspoon **lemon zest**

1 teaspoon **cumin**

1 **bay leaf**

1 bag **frozen chopped spinach**, thawed (8-12 ounces)

salt and pepper to taste

You can add chicken to this soup by cutting 1 pound of chicken tenders into 1 inch long chunks and adding them to the cooker before cooking under pressure. No need to adjust the cooking time!

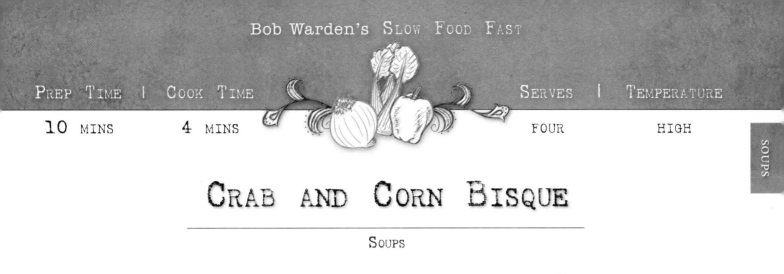

Prep Time	Cook Time	Serves	Temperature
10 MINS	4 MINS	FOUR	HIGH

SOUPS

CRAB AND CORN BISQUE

SOUPS

BISQUE IS MORE THAN JUST A FANCY NAME for soup. It describes this thick, creamy, steaming goodness you can achieve in your very own kitchen, no French chefs required.

1. HEAT butter in pressure cooker on high or "brown" with lid off until melted.

2. ADD onion and carrots and sauté 2-3 minutes until onions begin to turn translucent.

3. COVER with remaining ingredients, except for creamed corn and heavy cream, securely lock on the pressure cooker's lid, set the cooker to high and cook for 4 minutes.

4. PERFORM a quick release to release the cooker's pressure. Safely remove lid and use a slotted spoon to spoon out and transfer onions, carrots and crab meat to a blender or food processor. Blend until smooth.

SHOPPING LIST

4 tablespoons **butter or margarine**

1 **onion**, diced

4 **carrots**, peeled and sliced into 1/8 inch discs

2 teaspoons **chicken base** (see page: 12) mixed into 2 cups water

1/2 pound **lump crabmeat**

1 tablespoon **lemon juice**

1/4 cup **dry sherry**

1/2 teaspoon **paprika**

1 can **creamed corn** (14-16 ounces)

1/2 cup **heavy cream** (may use half and half)

salt and pepper to taste

additional **lump crabmeat**, for garnish

5. RETURN onion, carrot and crab mixture to the broth in the pot. Stir in creamed corn and heavy cream. If bisque cools down too much, set cooker to high or "brown" with the lid off to bring it back up to a simmer. Salt and pepper to taste and serve topped with a spoonful of lump crabmeat.

Bob's Tips

Use fresh crab if possible and prepare yourself for a luscious treat. Replace the chicken base with 2 cups of regular water and cook the crab, in the shell, while following the rest of the recipe. Remove crabmeat from shells before blending in step 4.

Prep Time	Cook Time		Serves	Temperature
10 MINS	15 MINS		SIX	LOW

SOUPS

CINNAMON SPICED TURKEY CHILI

Soups

This turkey chili is a new winter favorite of mine for those snow covered days when a cup of cinnamon spiced cider just isn't enough. The earthy aromas and complex flavors work so well, you'd never even know it was pretty good for you too!

1. Add the vegetable oil to the pressure cooker and heat on high or "brown" with the lid off. Add the ground turkey, breaking it up with a wooden spoon as it browns.

2. Once the turkey is browning well, add the chopped onion and minced garlic and cook for 3 additional minutes. Drain off half of the liquid in cooker.

3. Add the remaining ingredients and stir. Securely lock on the pressure cooker's lid, set the cooker to low and cook for 15 minutes.

3. Let the pressure release naturally for 10 minutes before quick releasing the remaining pressure. Safely remove lid and serve with a dollop of sour cream.

SHOPPING LIST

1 tablespoon **vegetable oil**

2 pounds **ground turkey**

1 **onion**, chopped large

1 tablespoon **minced garlic**

2 **red bell peppers**, chopped large

1 15 ounces can **diced tomatoes**, with liquid

1 14 ounces can **red kidney beans**, with liquid

1 1/2 teaspoons **chicken base** (see page: 12) mixed into 1 1/2 cups water

1 6 ounces can **tomato paste**

2 teaspoons **celery salt**

2 teaspoons **sugar**

1 teaspoon **cumin**

2 tablespoons **corn meal**

1 teaspoon **ground cinnamon**

1 teaspoon **coriander**

1 teaspoon **chili powder**

1/4 teaspoon **ground black pepper**

sour cream, for garnish

Bob's Tips I like to blend fresh cilantro into my sour cream to take the garnish to the next level. If you have a few extra cans around, black or white beans can be used in place of the kidney beans.

Prep Time	Cook Time		Serves	Temperature
10 MINS	35 MINS		SIX	HIGH

Black Bean Soup

SOUPS

The cilantro is what really takes this soup to the next level. It is similar in appearance to parsley, but definitely different in flavor. Add cumin, chili powder and lime juice and you're eating black beans as you'll swear they were always meant to be.

1. Heat oil, garlic, celery, onion and bell pepper in pressure cooker on high or "brown" with lid off for about 7 minutes, stirring frequently, until onions are translucent.

2. Rinse the dry black beans well and then add them to the cooker.

3. Cover with remaining ingredients, except for sour cream and securely lock on the pressure cooker's lid. Set the cooker to high and cook for 35 minutes.

4. Let the pressure release naturally for 15 minutes before quick releasing the remaining pressure and safely removing lid.

5. Use a potato masher, or the back of a large serving spoon to mash black beans against the bottom and walls of the cooker until two thirds of the beans are broken up, thickening the soup. (You can also use a slotted spoon to transfer two thirds of the beans to a food processor or blender to puree and then add back into the soup.)

6. Salt and pepper to taste and serve topped with sour cream.

Shopping List

2 tablespoons **vegetable oil**

1 tablespoon **minced garlic**

1 stalk **celery**, chopped small

1 **yellow onion**, diced

1 **red bell pepper**, chopped

1 pound **black beans**, uncooked

4 teaspoons **beef base** (see page: 12) mixed into 4 cups water

1 cup **water**

2 tablespoons **lime juice**

1 **bay leaf**

1 tablespoon **fresh cilantro**, chopped

1 teaspoon **cumin**

1 teaspoon **chili powder**

1 tablespoon **light brown sugar**

salt and pepper to taste

sour cream, for garnish

Bob's Tips If you can find one, pick up an old fashioned, red plastic ketchup squirt bottle (that you used to see at picnics and that you fill yourself) to fill with the sour cream garnish. This will allow you to make designs on the top of the soup as seen in the picture at left.

Prep Time	Cook Time	Serves	Temperature
5 MINS	10 MINS	SIX	HIGH

SOUPS

Split Pea and Bacon Soup

Soups

Just as it works its magic on green beans, the salty and hickory smoked taste of bacon brings out a wonderful sweetness in this split pea soup. So split a loaf of crusty bread and take this recipe for a dip.

1. Add all ingredients to pressure cooker and fill with enough water to cover everything by 1 1/2 inches. Stir well, until chicken base has dissolved. Securely lock on the pressure cooker's lid, set the cooker to high and cook for 10 minutes.

2. Let the pressure release naturally for 10 minutes before performing a quick release to release the remaining pressure. Safely remove lid and use a slotted spoon to scoop out 1 cup of the cooked split peas.

Shopping List

2 tablespoons **butter or margarine**

1 tablespoon **minced garlic**

1 **onion**, diced

2 **carrots**, peeled and diced

1 pound **dried split peas**

1 cup **cooked bacon pieces** (sold precooked in the salad dressing aisle)

3 teaspoons **chicken base** (see page: 12)

1 **bay leaf**

3. Blend the cup of split peas in blender or food processor until smooth, adding liquid to the soup if too thick.

4. Reintroduce blended peas to the cooking pot, mixing until well combined. Serve immediately.

Bob's Tips

Try adding 1 cup of frozen peas after the initial cooking has finished, stirring in and letting them sit for 2 minutes to heat through. You'll get all the flavors of traditional split pea soup with the crisp, sweet and fresh crunch of green peas.

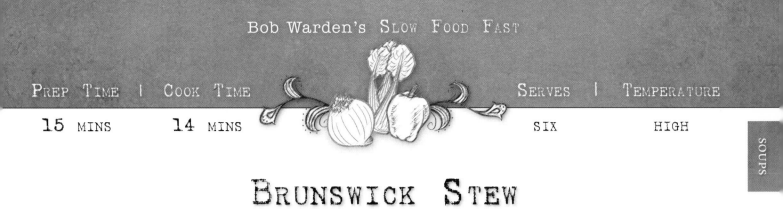

SOUPS

Prep Time	Cook Time		Serves	Temperature
15 MINS	14 MINS		SIX	HIGH

BRUNSWICK STEW

SOUPS

I WON'T ASK YOU TO BE COMPLETELY authentic and use rabbit (or this other small animal) meat in this stew, chicken and ham work just fine. With heaps of meat, lima beans and corn; if you don't have more meat and vegetables than broth, you don't have Brunswick stew!

1. ADD the butter, ham, garlic, onion, and bell pepper and to pressure cooker and cook on high or "brown" with lid off until ham begins to brown and onions are translucent.

2. COAT chicken leg quarters with the flour on all sides before adding them to the cooker.

3. ADD the remaining ingredients, except lima beans and corn, and securely lock on the pressure cooker's lid. Set the cooker to high and cook for 14 minutes.

4. LET the pressure release naturally for 10 minutes before quick releasing the remaining pressure and safely removing the lid. Remove chicken legs and set aside to cool for 5 minutes.

5. SET cooker to high or "brown" with lid off and stir lima beans and corn into stew.

6. SHRED chicken meat off of the bone using two forks. Discard bones and return meat to the stew. Salt and pepper to taste before serving.

SHOPPING LIST

2 tablespoons **butter**

1/2 pound **smoked (country) ham**, diced

1 tablespoon **minced garlic**

1 **onion**, chopped large

1 **green bell pepper**, chopped large

2 pounds **chicken leg quarters**

1 cup **flour**, to dredge chicken

2 cans **diced tomatoes** (14-16 ounces each)

3 teaspoons **chicken base** (see page: 12) mixed into 3 cups water

2 **bay leaves**

1 1/2 cups **lima beans**, frozen

1 1/2 cups **corn kernels**, frozen

salt and pepper to taste

Many variations of Brunswick Stew are made with smoked meat for a really downhome taste. This is easily replicated by adding a teaspoon or two of liquid smoke before cooking!

PREP TIME	COOK TIME	SERVES	TEMPERATURE
10 MINS	6 MINS	SIX	HIGH

CREAM OF CHICKEN SOUP WITH GNOCCHI DUMPLINGS

SOUPS

THIS CREAM OF CHICKEN SOUP RECIPE takes a totally original and delicious turn with the addition of Italian gnocchi dumplings. Now available in almost every grocery store's dry pasta aisle, gnocchi are small potato dumplings that cook up as large and satisfying as a traditional dumpling without all the work!

1. HEAT butter in pressure cooker on high or "brown" until melted.

2. COAT chicken thigh cubes with the flour on all sides before adding them and the celery to the cooker, sautéing for 2-3 minutes until chicken is lightly browned.

3. COVER with remaining ingredients, except for heavy cream.

4. SECURELY lock on the pressure cooker's lid, set the cooker to high and cook for 6 minutes.

SHOPPING LIST

3 tablespoons **butter or margarine**

1 pound **chicken tenders**, cubed

3 tablespoons **flour**

2 stalks **celery**, diced small

4 teaspoons **chicken base** (see page: 12) mixed into 4 cups water

16 ounces dry **gnocchi dumplings** (sold in pasta aisle)

1 sprig **fresh thyme** or 1 teaspoon dried

1 **bay leaf**

1 teaspoon **onion powder**

1 tablespoon **parsley flakes**

3/4 cup **heavy cream** (may use half and half)

salt and pepper to taste

5. PERFORM a quick release to release the cooker's pressure. Safely remove lid and slowly stir in the heavy cream. Salt and pepper to taste and serve immediately.

Bob's Tips

For firmer, more pasta-like gnocchi, add them with the heavy cream after the pressure cooking process. Switch the cooker to high or "brown" with lid off and boil for 3 to 4 minutes until gnocchi begin to float.

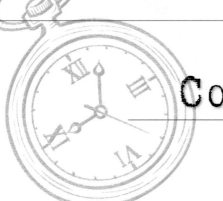

COOKING TIMES
BEEF

WHEN COOKING BEEF, browning the meat first will add more flavor, especially to the gravy. Letting the pressure release naturally for at least 10 minutes is recommended unless cooking thin cuts of meat.

BEEF	SIZE	LIQUID	COOK MINUTES	TEMP
BRISKET	2-3 pounds	covered	45	high
BRISKET	4-5 pounds	covered	70	high
CHUCK ROAST	3-4 pounds	2 cups	60	high
CORNED BEEF	2-3 pounds	covered	45	high
CORNED BEEF	4-5 pounds	covered	70	high
FLANK STEAK	2-3 pounds	1 cup	35	high
GROUND BEEF	1-2 pounds	1 cup	6	high
OXTAILS	any	covered	45	high
RIB ROAST	3-4 pounds	2 cups	60	high
ROUND ROAST	3-4 pounds	2 cups	60	high
SHANKS	2 inch thick	1 1/2 cups	45	high
SHORT RIBS	any	1 1/2 cups	30	high
SHOULDER ROAST	3-4 pounds	2 cups	60	high
STEW MEAT	1 inch cubes	1 cup	20	high
THIN STEAKS	less than 1 inch	2/3 cup	15	high

BEEF

Prep Time	Cook Time		Serves	Temperature
15 MINS	45 MINS		SIX	HIGH

PERFECT POT ROAST

Beef

No stranger to a pressure cooker, it's safe to say that I've made my fair share of pot roasts. Quite simply, this is the easiest way to prepare one without sacrificing a lick of flavor. Fork tender and a slow roasted flavor that's out of this world in an amazingly quick 45 minute cooking time!

1. Add the oil to the pressure cooker and heat on high or "brown" with the lid off.

2. Sprinkle the top of the roast with half of the celery salt, onion powder and a small pinch of ground black pepper.

3. Place the roast, seasoned side down in pressure cooker to brown. Sprinkle the remaining celery salt, onion powder and another small pinch of pepper over top as the bottom browns. Once the bottom has seared until dark brown and almost crusty, flip the roast and sear other side.

4. Pour in red wine, stab roast with a meat fork and push the meat around the bottom of the pan to release the glaze you've created.

5. Add the beef base, garlic, thyme, bay leaves and salt. Securely lock on the pressure cooker's lid, set the cooker to high and cook for 40 minutes.

SHOPPING LIST

Roast
4 tablespoons **vegetable oil**
2-3 pound **beef chuck roast**
1/2 teaspoon **celery salt**
1/2 teaspoon **onion powder**
ground black pepper
1/2 cup **red wine**
2 teaspoons **beef base** (see page: 12) mixed into 2 cups water
2 tablespoons **minced garlic**
1 sprig **fresh thyme**, or 1 teaspoon dried
2 **bay leaves**
1 teaspoon **salt**
Vegetables
6 small **redskin potatoes**, halved
2 small **onions**, peeled and quartered
2 cups **baby carrots**
2 stalks **celery**, cut into 1 inch pieces
2 tablespoons **corn starch**, optional

6. Perform a quick release to release the cooker's pressure. Safely remove lid and add the vegetables. Re-lock the pressure cooker's lid, set the cooker to high and cook for 5 additional minutes.

7. Perform a quick release to release the cooker's pressure. Serve covered in the au jus from cooker. To thicken the juices into gravy: combine the corn starch with 2 tablespoons water in a small dish and stir into cooker on high or "brown" with the lid off until thick.

Bob's Tips

Pot roast can be prepared in advance and refrigerated in an airtight container for up to five days.

Prep Time	Cook Time		Serves	Temperature
10 MINS	6 MINS		SIX	HIGH

GROUND BEEF STROGANOFF

Beef

While stroganoff is traditionally made with strips or cubes of beef, I've been eating this ground beef variation for as long as I can remember. With a sour cream and mushroom sauce, it's just one of those hearty family classics that reminds you why it's always a good idea to keep a pound of ground beef on hand.

1. Add the butter to the pressure cooker and heat on high or "brown" with the lid off until sizzling. Add the ground beef, breaking it up with spoon or spatula as it browns.

2. Once the ground beef is breaking up well, carefully drain most of the fat from the pot, and then add the onion and celery. Stir for 2 minutes until onions start to turn translucent.

SHOPPING LIST

1 tablespoon **butter or margarine**

1 pound **lean ground beef**

1/2 **onion**, diced

2 stalks **celery**, chopped

4 ounces **mushrooms**, sliced

1 teaspoon **beef base** (see page: 12) mixed into only 1/2 cup water

1/2 teaspoon **garlic powder**

1/2 teaspoon **onion powder**

1/4 teaspoon **allspice**

1 1/2 cups **reduced fat sour cream**

salt and pepper to taste

egg noodles, cooked separately

3. Add the remaining ingredients, except for the sour cream and egg noodles. Securely lock on the pressure cooker's lid, set the cooker to high and cook for 6 minutes.

4. Let the pressure release naturally for 10 minutes before quick releasing the remaining pressure and safely removing lid. Stir in sour cream, salt and pepper to taste and serve over egg noodles.

Egg noodles cook so fast that you can easily boil them on the stove as soon as the stroganoff is cooking in the pressure cooker and everything should come out at the same time.

PREP TIME	COOK TIME		SERVES	TEMPERATURE
10 MINS	5 MINS		SIX	HIGH

SWEET AND SOUR MEATBALLS

Beef

NEXT TIME YOU FIND YOURSELF volunteered to bring a main dish for a potluck, make these easy and tasty meatballs. They're the perfect party food and hold up well to reheating. With the effortless use of frozen meatballs, just don't tell anyone how you make them so perfectly round!

SHOPPING LIST

2 pounds (32 ounces) **frozen meatballs**

1/2 **onion**, diced

3/4 cup **water**

2/3 cup **light brown sugar**

1 cup **ketchup**

2 tablespoons **vinegar**

2 teaspoons **lemon juice**

2 tablespoons **soy sauce**

1. ADD all ingredients to pressure cooker, stir well and securely lock on lid. Set the cooker to high and cook for 5 minutes.

2. LET the pressure release naturally for 10 minutes before (carefully!) quick releasing the remaining pressure and safely removing lid. Serve over rice.

To make your own porcupine meatballs in place of the frozen meatballs: combine 1 pound ground beef with 1/2 cup uncooked long grain white rice, 1/2 cup water, 1/2 teaspoon onion powder, 1/4 teaspoon garlic powder and 1/4 teaspoon ground black pepper. Increase cooking time by 1 minute.

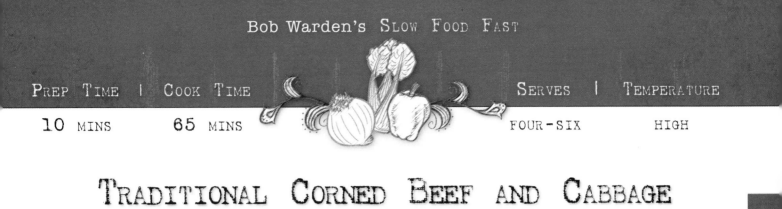

Prep Time	Cook Time		Serves	Temperature
10 MINS	65 MINS		FOUR-SIX	HIGH

Traditional Corned Beef and Cabbage

Beef

BEEF

YOU NO LONGER HAVE TO WAIT HALF A day for this Irish favorite! Corned beef can be found in both "point" and "flat" cuts. I suggest a flat cut, as points tend to vary greatly in thickness and contain more fat. Flat cuts also cut into nice even slices from one end to the other.

1. ADD corned beef, pickling spices, garlic and bay leaf to pressure cooker and cover with just enough water to sit parallel to the top of the beef.

2. SECURELY lock on the pressure cooker's lid, set the cooker to high and cook for 60 minutes.

SHOPPING LIST

2-3 pound **corned beef** with pickling spice packet

1 tablespoon **minced garlic**

1 bay leaf

<u>Vegetables</u>

6 small **redskin potatoes**, halved

2 cups **baby carrots**

1 small **head cabbage**, quartered

3. PERFORM a quick release to release the cooker's pressure. Safely remove lid and remove beef, letting it rest under tin foil for five minutes.

4. WHILE the beef is resting, add vegetables to the cooking liquid in pressure cooker, cabbage last. Securely lock on lid, set the cooker to high and cook for 5 minutes.

5. PERFORM a quick release to release the cooker's pressure. Slice corned beef against the meat's grain and serve with vegetables. If meat dries out, spoon a small amount of the cooking liquid over top to hydrate.

Bob's Tips To keep the pickling spices from getting in between the leaves of the cabbage, you can tie the spices into cheesecloth before dropping them into the pot. A stainless steel tea steeping ball also works well. If your beef does not come with a packet of spices, you can add 1 tablespoon of pickling spice, found in the spice aisle.

PREP TIME	COOK TIME		SERVES	TEMPERATURE
15 MINS	12 MINS		FOUR	HIGH

ORANGE PEPPER STEAK

Beef

BEEF

Though it's called Pepper Steak, this recipe is more citrus than spice and in only 12 minutes time, who needs those take out cartons? This no stir, stir fry is best served over white rice with a side of steamed broccoli.

1. ADD the sesame and vegetable oil to the pressure cooker and heat on high or "brown" with the lid off.

2. MIX the salt and pepper into the flour and generously coat the beef strips.

3. PLACE beef strips in pressure cooker and lightly brown on all sides.

4. ADD the remaining ingredients, except for the onion, green and red bell peppers and securely lock on the pressure cooker's lid. Set the cooker to high and cook for 8 minutes.

5. PERFORM a quick release to release the cooker's pressure. Safely remove lid and add the onions and peppers.

6. SECURELY lock on the pressure cooker's lid and cook on high for an additional 4 minutes.

7. PERFORM a quick release to release the cooker's pressure. Safely remove lid and serve topped with fresh orange slices.

SHOPPING LIST

1 tablespoon **sesame oil**

2 tablespoons **vegetable oil**

1 pound **beef round steaks**, cut into 1/2 inch strips

1 cup **flour**

1/2 teaspoon **salt**

1/2 teaspoon **pepper**

1 teaspoon **beef base** (see page: 12) mixed into 1 cup **orange juice**

2 teaspoons **minced garlic**

2 teaspoons **fresh orange zest**

3 tablespoons **soy sauce**

2 tablespoons **sugar**

1/2 **white onion**, peeled and sliced in 1/2 inch wide strips

1 **green bell pepper**, cored and sliced in 1/2 inch wide strips

1 **red bell pepper**, cored and sliced in 1/2 inch wide strips

fresh orange slices, for garnish

Bob's Tips

Though you are zesting a fresh orange, it's best to buy store-bought orange juice for the juice in this recipe. It's much more concentrated than fresh and adds a better flavor. Slice the fresh orange for the garnish!

Prep Time	Cook Time	Serves	Temperature
10 MINS	60 MINS	FOUR-SIX	HIGH

BEEF

BEEF BRISKET ROAST

Beef

LONG, SLOW COOKING IS USUALLY THE KEY to this inexpensive cut of meat. Really long and really slow cooking, sometimes as long as eight or ten hours! A flavorful cut, in only 60 minutes under pressure, you no longer have to wait all day to get your money's worth!

1. ADD brisket to pressure cooker and cover with remaining ingredients, except corn starch.

2. SECURELY lock on the pressure cooker's lid, set the cooker to high and cook for 60 minutes.

3. LET the pressure release naturally for 10 minutes before quick releasing the remaining pressure and safely removing lid.

SHOPPING LIST

2-3 pound **brisket**

1 teaspoon **beef base** (see page: 12) mixed into 1 cup water

2 cups **water**

1 tablespoon **minced garlic**

1 packet **powdered onion soup mix**

1 **bay leaf**

1 sprig **fresh thyme** or 1 teaspoon dried

2 tablespoons **corn starch**

salt and pepper to taste

4. REMOVE brisket and set aside to rest under tin foil as you thicken the gravy. To thicken gravy: set the cooker to high or "brown" with lid off until cooking juices are simmering. Mix corn starch with 2 tablespoons water and slowly add to simmering juices, stirring constantly, until thick.

5. CARVE brisket thin, against the meat's grain and serve smothered in gravy.

To add vegetables: perform a quick release 55 minutes into the cooking time to cover brisket with large chunks of your favorite vegetables such as celery, carrots or halved new potatoes. Re-secure lid and cook for 5 minutes on high before letting the pressure release naturally and following the rest of the recipe.

Prep Time	Cook Time		Serves	Temperature
10 MINS	15 MINS		FOUR	HIGH

STEAK DIANE

BEEF

BEEF

STEAK DIANE'S UNBEATABLE FLAVOR comes from the unbeatable combination of beef, butter, Worcestershire sauce and mustard powder. While typically made with beef tenderloin or filet mignon, the pressure cooker cooks far less expensive cuts of meat just as tender!

1. ADD the butter and garlic to the pressure cooker and heat on high or "brown" with the lid off until sizzling.

2. PLACE steaks in pressure cooker and lightly brown on both sides.

3. ADD the beef base mixed with water, Worcestershire sauce, dry mustard and onion powder and securely lock on the pressure cooker's lid. Set the cooker to high and cook for 15 minutes.

SHOPPING LIST

2 tablespoons **butter**

1 teaspoon **minced garlic**

4 beef **round steaks**, about 3/4 inch thick

1/2 teaspoon **beef base** (see page: 12) mixed into 1/2 cup water

1 tablespoon **Worcestershire sauce**

1/2 teaspoon **dry mustard powder**

1/4 teaspoon **onion powder**

1 tablespoon **brandy**

1/3 cup **heavy cream**

1 tablespoon **chives**, chopped

1 tablespoon **parsley flakes**

salt and pepper to taste

4. PERFORM a quick release to release the cooker's pressure before safely removing lid and adding the remaining ingredients. Stir until well combined and serve with favorite potato dish.

This recipe is a bare bones version of the dish, ready for all kinds of quick and easy additions. Try adding 1/2 of a diced red onion, or 2 to 3 diced shallots while browning the meat and 8 ounces of halved mushrooms with the remaining ingredients for something even better!

PREP TIME	COOK TIME		SERVES	TEMPERATURE
5 MINS	7 MINS		SIX	HIGH

BEEF

SWEDISH MEATBALLS

BEEF

WITH ALMOST NO PREP TIME AND ONLY a 7 minute cook time, these Swedish meatballs in sour cream gravy are "fast" food your family can really get behind. While you can make the meatballs yourself (see my tips below), the sour cream sauce is so rich with the flavors of traditional Swedish meatballs that using frozen meatballs of any variety saves you time without compromising any taste. Plus, they easily stack on top of each other in the pressure cooker without losing their shape.

SHOPPING LIST

2 pounds (32 ounces) **frozen meatballs**

2 teaspoons **beef base** (see page: 12) mixed into 2 cups water

2 teaspoons **minced garlic**

1 1/2 teaspoons **onion powder**

1/4 teaspoon **nutmeg**

1/2 teaspoon **allspice**

1 tablespoon **parsley flakes**

16 ounces **sour cream**

salt and pepper to taste

1. ADD all ingredients, except for sour cream, to pressure cooker and securely lock on lid. Set the cooker to high and cook for 7 minutes.

2. PERFORM a quick release to release the cooker's pressure. Safely remove lid and immediately stir in the sour cream until well blended. Salt and pepper to taste and serve immediately over egg noodles or alongside mashed or fingerling potatoes.

To make your own, fresh meatballs: combine 1 cup white breadcrumbs with 1/2 cup heavy cream and let sit 5 minutes. Mix into 1 pound lean ground beef, and then add 2 teaspoons onion powder, 2 tablespoons parsley, 2 teaspoons salt, 1/2 teaspoon pepper and 1/8 teaspoon nutmeg.

PREP TIME	COOK TIME	SERVES	TEMPERATURE
15 MINS	45 MINS	SIX	HIGH

CHIANTI POT ROAST WITH MUSHROOMS AND TOMATOES

BEEF

BEEF

THIS TWIST ON A CLASSIC POT ROAST RECIPE is like booking a one-way ticket to Tuscany, except it only takes an hour for your taste buds to make it there and you don't have to change planes twice or get on an airplane at all. The slightly sweet Chianti sauce is a welcome change of pace to any dinner routine.

1. ADD the oil to the pressure cooker and heat on high or "brown" with the lid off.

2. SPRINKLE both sides of the roast with the salt, garlic powder and a pinch of black pepper and then place the roast in pressure cooker to brown. Sear both sides until dark brown and almost crusty.

3. POUR in 3/4 cup Chianti, stab roast with a meat fork and push the meat around the bottom of the pan to release the glaze you've created.

4. ADD the beef base, tomato paste, sugar, minced garlic and Italian seasoning. Securely lock on the pressure cooker's lid, set the cooker to high and cook for 45 minutes.

5. PERFORM a quick release to release the cooker's pressure. Safely remove lid, and then remove the roast to rest under tin foil.

6. ADD mushrooms and tomatoes to pressure cooker and cook over high heat, lid off for 3-5 minutes before stirring in remaining 3/4 cup Chianti. To thicken the sauce: combine the corn starch with 2 tablespoons water in a small dish and stir into the simmering sauce and vegetables until thick. Serve over roast.

SHOPPING LIST

Roast
4 tablespoons **olive oil**
2-3 pound **beef chuck roast**
1/2 teaspoon **salt**
1/2 teaspoon **garlic powder**
ground black pepper
1 1/2 cups **Chianti red wine**, split into two 3/4 cup portions
1 1/2 teaspoons **beef base** (see page: 12) mixed into 1 1/2 cups water
3 ounces **tomato paste** (1/2 small can)
2 teaspoons **sugar**
2 tablespoons **minced garlic**
1 1/2 teaspoons Italian seasoning
Vegetables
8 ounces **baby bella mushrooms**, sliced (sold pre-sliced in many stores)
4 medium **tomatoes**, cut in large chunks
2 tablespoons **corn starch**

Believe it or not, this recipe goes great with cheese tortellini! You can buy fresh tortellini in the refrigerated section of your grocery store and add them, as well as an extra tablespoon of beef base mixed with 1 cup water for them to absorb, to the sauce in the pressure cooker when you add the mushrooms and tomatoes, cooking 6-8 minutes until they are tender.

Prep Time	Cook Time		Serves	Temperature
15 MINS	15 MINS		FOUR	HIGH

BEEF GOULASH

Beef

GOULASH IS ONE OF THE BEST AND certainly one of the most recognizable dishes that Hungary has given us. While closely related to good old American beef stew, it's the paprika that really sets this dish apart.

1. ADD the butter and bacon to the pressure cooker and heat on high or "brown" with the lid off until bacon begins to crisp.

2. PLACE garlic and beef cubes in pressure cooker and lightly brown on all sides.

3. ADD the remaining ingredients and securely lock on the pressure cooker's lid. Set the cooker to high and cook for 15 minutes.

4. LET the pressure release naturally for 5 minutes before quick releasing the remaining pressure and safely removing lid.

5. To THICKEN: set the pressure cooker to high or "brown" with lid off. Combine the corn starch with 2 tablespoons water in a small dish and stir into the simmering goulash until thick. Salt and pepper to taste and serve over egg noodles or spaetzle.

SHOPPING LIST

1 tablespoon **butter**

2 slices **raw bacon**, diced

1 tablespoon **minced garlic**

1 pound **beef round steaks**, cut into 3/4 inch cubes

1 **red onion**, diced

1 **red bell pepper**, chopped

1 **green bell pepper**, chopped

2 teaspoons **beef base** (see page: 12) mixed into 2 cups water

3 tablespoons **tomato paste**

zest of **1/2 lemon**

1 teaspoon **dried marjoram**

2 teaspoons **paprika**

1 teaspoon **caraway seeds**

2 tablespoons **corn starch**

salt and pepper to taste

Hungarian or sweet paprika works best in this recipe, but regular paprika will do. Stewed vegetables such as carrots and potatoes work well in this dish. Cut them into large chunks and interrupt the cooking process with a quick release to add them in 5 minutes before goulash is finished cooking.

Prep Time	Cook Time	Serves	Temperature
15 MINS	30 MINS	SIX	HIGH

Wine Braised Short Ribs with Prunes

Beef

BEEF

When it comes to short ribs, I'm here to say that the buck does not stop at barbecue sauce. Very versatile, these ribs are not to be sold *short*. These wine braised ribs stew alongside prunes for a deep and somewhat fruity flavor that's out of this world!

1. Add the vegetable oil to the pressure cooker and heat on high or "brown" with the lid off until sizzling.

2. Place short ribs in pressure cooker and lightly brown on both sides.

3. Cover with the remaining ingredients and securely lock on the pressure cooker's lid. Set the cooker to high and cook for 30 minutes.

Shopping List

2 tablespoons **vegetable oil**

3-4 pounds **short ribs**, trimmed of fat and seasoned with a pinch of salt and pepper

1 **onion**, halved then sliced 1/4 inch thick

1 cup **dry red wine**

1 teaspoon **beef base** (see page: 12) mixed into 1 cup water

3 tablespoons **tomato paste**

1 tablespoon **minced garlic**

1 teaspoon **Worcestershire sauce**

12 pitted prunes

1 bay leaf

1 teaspoon **dried thyme**

salt and pepper to taste

4. Let the pressure release naturally for 10 minutes before quick releasing the remaining pressure and safely removing lid. Salt and pepper to taste and serve.

Bob's Tips

This recipe is also great with an extremely dark beer in place of the red wine. I like to use Guinness as it's just about as dark as beer gets!

Prep Time		Cook Time			Serves		Temperature
10 MINS		8 MINS			SIX		HIGH

SLOPPY JOES

BEEF

BEEF

SLOPPY JOES ARE ABOUT AS COMFORT food as a sandwich gets. Like macaroni and cheese is to pasta—Sloppy Joes are to sandwiches—simple, satisfying, and something the whole family will enjoy. Serve them alongside that macaroni and cheese and take a trip down memory lane!

1. ADD the vegetable oil to the pressure cooker and heat on high or "brown" with the lid off until sizzling. Add the ground beef, breaking it up with spoon or spatula as it browns.

2. ONCE the ground beef is breaking up well, carefully drain most of the fat from the pot, and then add the diced onion. Stir in for 2 minutes until onions start to turn translucent.

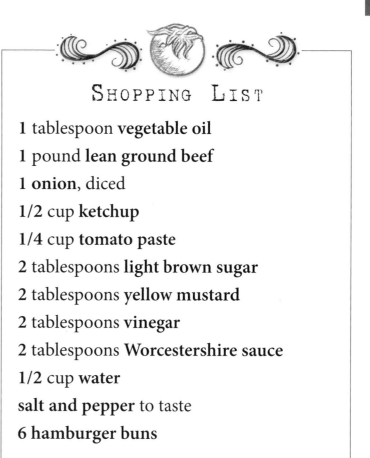

SHOPPING LIST

1 tablespoon **vegetable oil**

1 pound **lean ground beef**

1 **onion**, diced

1/2 cup **ketchup**

1/4 cup **tomato paste**

2 tablespoons **light brown sugar**

2 tablespoons **yellow mustard**

2 tablespoons **vinegar**

2 tablespoons **Worcestershire sauce**

1/2 cup **water**

salt and pepper to taste

6 hamburger buns

3. ADD the remaining ingredients, except hamburger buns and stir. Securely lock on the pressure cooker's lid, set the cooker to high and cook for 8 minutes.

4. LET the pressure release naturally for 10 minutes before quick releasing the remaining pressure and safely removing lid. Salt and pepper to taste and serve on hamburger buns.

Bob's Tips

Try to purchase nice, large and dense hamburger buns to hold up to a generous amount of the wonderful Sloppy Joe sauce. Lightly toast buns and top with cheddar cheese for that little extra touch.

Prep Time	Cook Time			Serves	Temperature
15 MINS	20 MINS			SIX	HIGH

BEEF

Beef and Barley Stew

Beef

A COLD WINTER NIGHT IS MUCH MORE bearable when you know you have a steaming hot bowl of beef stew to come home to. Even the smell as you walk in the door will warm you up. Pair this with some crusty French bread or even cornbread and let it snow!

1. ADD all ingredients except peas, onion, mushrooms and corn starch to the pressure cooker and securely lock on the lid. Set the cooker to high and cook for 20 minutes.

2. LET the pressure release naturally for 5 minutes before quick releasing the remaining pressure and safely removing the lid.

3. SET cooker to high or "brown" with lid off and add peas, onion and mushrooms. Simmer for 5 minutes.

4. POUR corn starch mixture into simmering stew slowly until stew thickens to your liking. Salt and pepper to taste and serve.

SHOPPING LIST

2 pounds **chuck or round roast**, cut into 1 1/2 inch cubes

1 cup **baby carrots**

2 stalks **celery**, cut into 1 1/2 inch pieces

1/3 cup **pearled barley**

1 tablespoon **olive oil**

4 teaspoons **beef base** (see page: 12) mixed into 4 cups water

1/2 cup **red wine**

2 tablespoons **tomato paste**

1/8 teaspoon **ground allspice**

1 tablespoon **minced garlic**

2 **bay leaves**

1 sprig **fresh thyme**, or 1 teaspoon dried

1 cup **frozen peas**

1 **onion**, peeled and sliced thin

8 ounces **mushrooms**, halved

2 tablespoons **corn starch**, mixed into 2 tablespoons water

salt and pepper to taste

For a more traditional beef stew, replace the pearled barley with 8 halved new potatoes, or try adding 2 cups diced turnips. If serving with a crusty French bread, heat an oven to 400 degrees and cook bread on rack for 5 minutes to crisp up the outside while warming the inside.

Prep Time	Cook Time	Serves	Temperature
10 MINS	50 MINS	FOUR-SIX	HIGH

BBQ Brisket

Beef

BEEF

BRING THIS BBQ BRISKET TO YOUR NEXT picnic and you'll be sure to make more than a few friends and for good reason—just don't host the picnic in your backyard—you'll confuse your guests as to where you're hiding the smokehouse!

1. ADD brisket to pressure cooker and cover with remaining ingredients.

2. SECURELY lock on the pressure cooker's lid, set the cooker to high and cook for 50 minutes.

SHOPPING LIST

2-3 pound **brisket**

1 batch **Stick to Your Ribs BBQ Sauce**, recipe: page 187

1 can or bottle **beer**

2 teaspoons **liquid smoke**

3. PERFORM a quick release to release the cooker's pressure. Safely remove lid and remove beef, letting it rest under tin foil for five minutes.

4. SLICE brisket against the meat's grain and serve smothered in sauce from cooker. Serve with your picnic favorites!

Bob's Tips

If you are in a pinch you can substitute a bottle of your favorite barbecue sauce in place of the Stick to Your Ribs BBQ Sauce... don't worry, I'll look the other way!

Prep Time	Cook Time		Serves	Temperature
15 MINS	15 MINS		FOUR	HIGH

BEEF

Beef Burgundy

Beef

This traditional French dish, also known as Beef Bourguignon has been a favorite of mine for as long as I can remember. Though the recipe has changed over the years, the key to all of its great flavors is still the same; browning the meat in butter and bacon fat before stewing it in wine.

1. ADD the butter, bacon and garlic to the pressure cooker and heat on high or "brown" with the lid off until bacon begins to crisp.

2. COMBINE the salt and pepper with flour and evenly coat beef cubes on all sides.

3. PLACE beef cubes in pressure cooker and lightly brown on all sides.

4. ADD the remaining ingredients, except 3/4 cup of the Burgundy and the corn starch and securely lock on the pressure cooker's lid. Set the cooker to high and cook for 15 minutes.

5. PERFORM a quick release to release the cooker's pressure before safely removing lid and stirring in remaining 3/4 cup Burgundy.

6. To THICKEN the sauce: set the pressure cooker to high or "brown" with lid off. Combine the corn starch with 2 tablespoons water in a small dish and stir into the simmering sauce until thick. Salt and pepper to taste and serve over egg noodles, your favorite pasta or potato dish.

SHOPPING LIST

2 tablespoons **butter**

2 slices **raw bacon**, cut into 1/4 inch pieces

1 tablespoon **minced garlic**

1 pound **beef round steaks**, cut into 3/4 inch cubes

1 cup **flour,** mixed with a pinch of salt and pepper

1 1/2 cups **Burgundy or dry red wine**, split into two 3/4 cup portions

1 teaspoon **beef base** (see page: 12) mixed into 1 cup water

1 tablespoon **tomato paste**

8 ounces **mushrooms**, cleaned and halved

2 cups **white pearl onions**, peeled

1 teaspoon **dried tarragon**

1 **bay leaf**

2 tablespoons **corn starch**

salt and pepper to taste

Bob's Tips

Typically, the herbs in this dish would be prepared into a "bouquet garni"; a little bundle of the fresh herbs you have on hand, bound together with string for easy retrieval at the end of the cooking process.

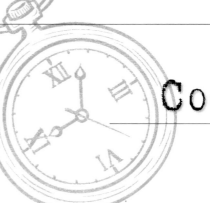

Cooking Times
Poultry

WHEN COOKING POULTRY, especially whole chickens or large turkey legs and breasts, be sure to use a meat thermometer after cooking to check that the internal temperature has reached 180 degrees. For better color and better tasting skin, brown the meat first.

Chicken	Size	Liquid	Cook Minutes	Temp
Breasts, bone in	any	1/2 cup	10	high
Breasts, boneless	any	1/2 cup	5	high
Cornish Hen	2 hens	1 cup	12	high
Legs	2 pounds	1/2 cup	7	high
Thighs	2 pounds	1/2 cup	7	high
Whole Chicken	3-4 pounds	2 cups	30	high
Wings	1-3 pounds	1/2 cup	7	high
Turkey				
Breast, bone in	3-5 pounds	2 cups	30	high
Breast, boneless	3-5 pounds	2 cups	25	high
Legs	2-4 legs	1 1/2 cups	17	high

POULTRY

Prep Time	Cook Time	Serves	Temperature
15 MINS	10 MINS	SIX	HIGH

CHICKEN PICCATA

POULTRY

This classic Italian dish is tangy, tart and delicious. In the pressure cooker, the rich, buttery, lemon and wine sauce infuses straight into the chicken for a 10 minute dinner that is bursting with all of the flavors of any fine restaurant.

1. DIP chicken breasts in lightly salted flour until they are well coated.

2. POUR the olive oil and butter into the pressure cooker and heat on high or "brown" with the lid off, until sizzling.

3. PLACE chicken breasts into pressure cooker, browning them on both sides.

4. ADD onions and garlic into cooker.

5. ONCE both sides of the chicken are browned and onions are beginning to sweat, add in remaining ingredients except corn starch, capers and lemon garnish.

6. SECURELY lock on the pressure cooker's lid, set to high and cook for 10 minutes.

SHOPPING LIST

6 small **boneless, skinless chicken breast halves** (about 2 pounds)

1/2 cup **flour**, mixed with pinch of salt

2 tablespoons **olive oil**

2 tablespoons **butter**

1/2 **red onion**, diced

1 tablespoon **minced garlic**

1 teaspoon **chicken base** (see page: 12) mixed into 1 cup water

1 cup **dry white wine**

1/4 cup **lemon juice**

1/4 teaspoon **white pepper**

1/2 teaspoon **Italian seasoning**

1 tablespoon **corn starch**

2 tablespoons **capers**, jarred

1 **lemon**, sliced thin, for garnish

7. Perform a quick release to release the cooker's pressure. Safely remove lid, then remove the chicken breasts and set aside.

8. THICKEN the cooking liquid into a sauce by combining the corn starch with 2 tablespoons water in a small dish and then stirring it into the cooker on high or brown, with lid off, until thick.

9. RETURN chicken into sauce to fully coat before serving. Serve topped with capers and fresh lemon slices.

Although store bought lemon juice is easiest, fresh squeezed lemon juice makes this recipe truly great. For a full meal, serve over well oiled angel hair pasta with a side of steamed asparagus or broccoli.

Prep Time	Cook Time		Serves	Temperature
15 MINS	10 MINS		FOUR	HIGH

Chicken Thigh Osso Buco

Poultry

POULTRY

Typically made with veal or lamb shanks, this recipe for Osso Buco substitutes far cheaper chicken thighs without sacrificing any of the incredible Italian flavors you'd expect. The added bonus is that the dish is suddenly very kid friendly when you've got a whole family to please!

1. Add the olive oil to the pressure cooker and heat on high or "brown" with the lid off.

2. Coat the chicken thighs in the seasoned flour before adding to cooker to lightly brown on both sides.

3. Add the garlic, onion, carrots and celery and sauté for 1 minute before covering with remaining ingredients.

4. Securely lock on the pressure cooker's lid, set the cooker to high and cook for 10 minutes.

5. Let the pressure release naturally for 10 minutes before quick releasing the remaining pressure and safely removing lid. Salt and pepper to taste and serve.

Shopping List

3 tablespoons **olive oil**

8 chicken thighs

1 cup **flour** mixed with a pinch of salt and pepper

1 **red onion**, chopped

2 tablespoons **minced garlic**

2 **carrots**, cut into 1/4 inch discs

2 stalks **celery**, chopped

1 teaspoon **chicken base** (see page: 12) mixed into 1/2 cup water

1 cup **dry red wine**

1 can **diced tomatoes** (14-16 ounces)

2 tablespoons **tomato paste**

2 teaspoons **Italian seasoning**

salt and pepper to taste

Bob's Tips

Though the meat will be more tender with bone-in thighs, this can also be prepared with boneless, skinless chicken thighs for easier eating! Try serving with the traditional Osso Buco gremolata topping, recipe on page: 109.

Prep Time	Cook Time		Serves	Temperature
15 MINS	14 MINS		FOUR	HIGH

Chicken with 40 Cloves of Garlic

Poultry

W HILE THIS RECIPE MAY AT FIRST SOUND like the kind of dish you'd want to avoid on a dinner date, the garlic cooks up mild and soft; almost buttery. The consensus is that you absolutely must serve this with thin, toasted slices of a crusty bread to literally spread the creamy garlic cloves onto.

1. ADD the olive oil and butter or margarine to the pressure cooker and heat on high or "brown" with the lid off, until sizzling.

2. DIP chicken pieces in seasoned flour until they are well coated and add to cooker, lightly browning on all sides.

3. COVER with remaining ingredients, securely lock on the pressure cooker's lid, set the cooker to high and cook for 14 minutes.

SHOPPING LIST

2 tablespoons **olive oil**

2 tablespoons **butter or margarine**

2 pounds **chicken pieces**, bone in

1/2 cup **flour**, mixed with 1/2 teaspoon salt and 1/2 teaspoon pepper

4 stalks **celery**, cut into 2 inch lengths

40 cloves **garlic**, peeled

1/2 teaspoon **chicken base** (see page: 12) mixed into 1/2 cup water

1/4 cup **dry white wine**

1/2 teaspoon **dried rosemary**

1 teaspoon **dried thyme**

salt and pepper to taste

4. LET the pressure release naturally for 10 minutes before quick releasing the remaining pressure and safely removing lid.

5. SALT and pepper chicken pieces to taste, serving them with tongs. Use a slotted spoon to serve celery and garlic cloves over top.

Most grocery stores sell garlic cloves that are already peeled and ready to go in a small plastic jar usually found in the produce department's refrigerated salad case. One whole jar should be just enough for this recipe.

POULTRY

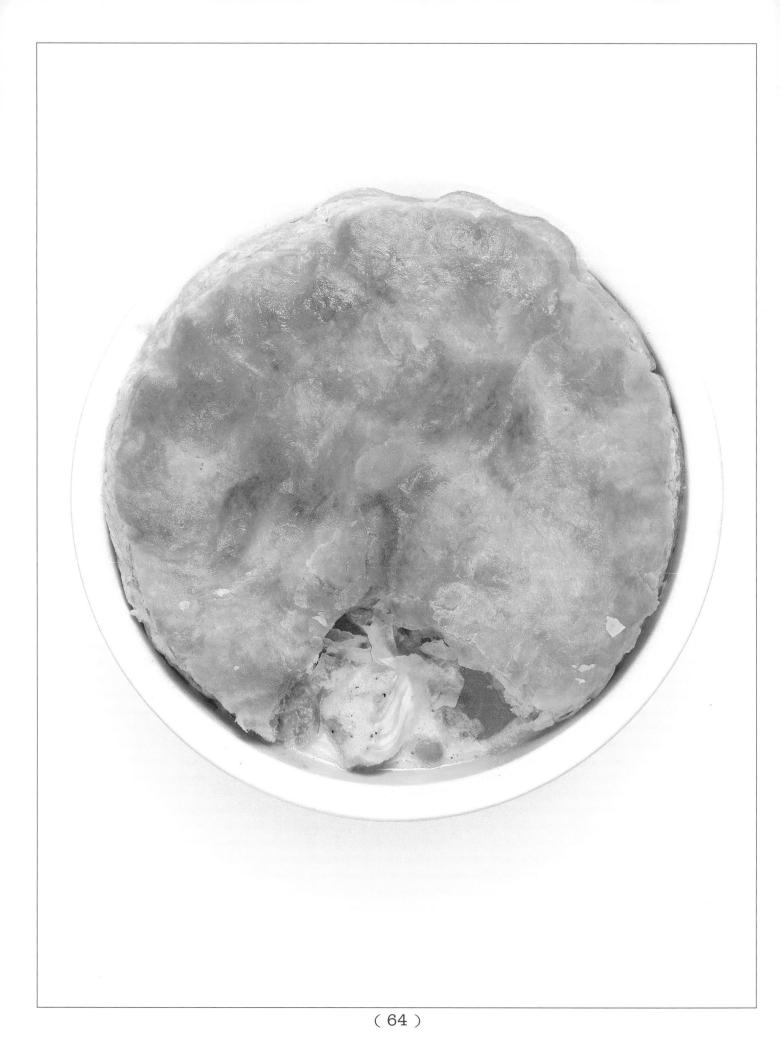

Prep Time	Cook Time	Serves	Temperature
25 MINS	5 MINS	FOUR	HIGH

CHICKEN POT PIE

POULTRY

THIS CHUNKY COMFORT FOOD CLASSIC can't be made any easier or faster than this! With a rich and flaky puff pastry "crown" you'll feel like a king dipping into the luxuriously creamy filling that is secretly thickened with instant mashed potatoes!

1. PREHEAT oven to 400 degrees. Spray a sheet pan well with nonstick cooking spray and lay out a sheet of puff pastry. Place the individual serving bowls you plan to serve the dish in upside down on the puff pastry sheet and use a paring knife to trace around the circumference of the bowl to cut out 4 circular pastry tops. Discard (or save for another time) excess pastry trimmings.

2. PLACE remaining ingredients, except Parmesan cheese, heavy cream, potato flakes and peas into pressure cooker and securely lock on the lid. Set the cooker to high and cook for 5 minutes.

3. WHILE the pot pie filling is cooking in the pressure cooker, place the baking sheet of circular pastry tops into the preheated oven and bake 8-12 minutes until golden brown.

SHOPPING LIST

1 package **frozen puff pastry sheets**, thawed
nonstick cooking spray
2 tablespoons **butter or margarine**
1 **onion**, chopped
3 **boneless, skinless chicken breasts**, cut into 3 strips then cubed
8 ounces **mushrooms**, sliced
2 **carrots**, cut into 1/4 inch discs
1 teaspoon **chicken base** (see page: 12) mixed into 1 cup water
4 **new red potatoes**, cubed
1/2 teaspoon **dried thyme**
1/2 teaspoon **poultry seasoning**
1 **bay leaf**
1 teaspoon **sugar**
3 tablespoons **Parmesan cheese**
1/2 cup **heavy cream**
4 tablespoons **instant potato flakes**
1 cup **frozen peas**, thawed
salt and pepper to taste

4. WHEN the filling is finished cooking, let the pressure release naturally for 5 minutes before quick releasing the remaining pressure and safely removing lid. Stir in the Parmesan cheese, heavy cream, potato flakes and peas until thick and creamy. Salt and pepper to taste and serve in individual bowls, each topped with a puff pastry top.

Bob's Tips

The trimmings left after cutting the circular puff pastry tops can be cut into small squares and baked into light and fluffy croutons to top any soup or salad!

POULTRY

Prep Time	Cook Time	Serves	Temperature
12 MINS	12 MINS	TWO-FOUR	HIGH

Cornish Game Hens with Garlic and Rosemary

Poultry

This classic roasting recipe is only missing one thing: the woe of waiting for a slow roasted dinner. I am here to report, however, that the flavors are all intact. The fragrant rosemary and intensely infused garlic is the perfect pair for this pair of Cornish hens and in only 12 minutes under pressure; the flavors would try to escape… if they had the time!

Shopping List

2 **Cornish game hens**, giblets removed
2 cloves **garlic**
2 wedges **lemon**

Cooking Liquid
1/2 teaspoon **chicken base** (see page: 12) mixed into 1/2 cup water
1/2 cup **dry white wine**
2 tablespoons **lemon juice**
1 tablespoon **butter or margarine**
1 teaspoon **poultry seasoning**

Herb Rub
2 tablespoons **olive oil**
2 tablespoons **minced garlic**
1 tablespoon **parsley flakes**
2 teaspoons **fresh rosemary leaves**
1/2 teaspoon **salt**
1/4 teaspoon **ground black pepper**

1. RINSE each Cornish hen well inside and out, then stuff cavity with 1 clove of garlic and 1 lemon wedge. Truss the back legs together with baking twine and tuck wings underneath body.

2. ADD the Cooking Liquid ingredients to the pressure cooker and (for best results) place a metal rack over top for the hens to keep above the water level. Place hens on rack.

3. MIX Herb Rub ingredients in a small bowl, using the back of a spoon to press ingredients into the bowl, releasing the natural oils of the rosemary.

4. THOROUGHLY coat the tops of the hens with the herb rub, securely lock on the pressure cooker's lid, set the cooker to high and cook for 12 minutes (15 if hens are very large).

5. LET the pressure release naturally for 10 minutes before quick releasing the remaining pressure and safely removing the lid. Let hens rest 5 minutes before serving.

Try making an herb rub out of a combination of fresh herbs, such as thyme, rosemary and sage. I make it a rule to crush any fresh herbs I have that are about to go bad into olive oil and keep the rub refrigerated. It extends the life of your fresh herbs for weeks!

Southwestern Ground Turkey Mac

POULTRY

POULTRY

THIS IS LIKE A GROWN UP VERSION OF A childhood favorite, one skillet meal. A little bit spicy, but a lot of bit cheesy and ready in only 7 minutes under pressure; the bell peppers and corn bring a fresh, crisp crunch you'd never find in a regular old chili mac.

1. ADD the vegetable oil to the pressure cooker and heat on high or "brown" with the lid off. Add the ground turkey, breaking it up with a wooden spoon as it browns.

2. ONCE the turkey is slightly browned, cover with remaining ingredients, except processed cheese, red bell pepper and corn. Securely lock on the pressure cooker's lid, set the cooker to high and cook for 7 minutes.

3. PERFORM a quick release to release the cooker's pressure. Safely remove lid and stir in the cheese, red bell pepper and corn until cheese is completely melted. Salt and pepper to taste and serve immediately.

SHOPPING LIST

1 tablespoon **vegetable oil**

1 pound **ground turkey**

2 1/2 cups **elbow macaroni**

1/2 **green bell pepper**, diced

2 teaspoons **chicken base** (see page: 12) mixed into 2 cups water

1/2 cup **water**

1/2 teaspoon **onion powder**

1/4 teaspoon **chili powder**

1/4 teaspoon **cayenne pepper**

2 tablespoons **butter or margarine**

3/4 pound **processed cheese**, cubed (such as Velveeta)

1/2 **red bell pepper**, diced small

1 cup **frozen corn kernels**

salt and pepper to taste

Bob's Tips

Shopping for ground turkey is a little trickier than shopping for ground beef, as the fat content of the ground is not always as clearly labeled. I like to use ground turkey with 6-12g of fat per serving, often labeled as "lean". Ground turkey breast, with only 1 or 2g of fat is usable but much drier. Watch out for full fat ground turkey with as much as 20g of fat, even more than ground beef!

Prep Time	Cook Time		Serves	Temperature
15 MINS	10 MINS		FOUR	HIGH

Chicken Cacciatore

Poultry

Literally translated from Italian, this "hunter-style" dish is an easy way to prepare most any cut of chicken with boundless flavor. When I was growing up, this was one of those weeknight dishes I asked for regularly, even if I couldn't pronounce the name!

1. Add the olive oil to the pressure cooker and heat on high or "brown" with the lid off until sizzling.

2. Coat the chicken breasts in the seasoned flour before adding to cooker skin side down to lightly brown.

3. Add the remaining ingredients, except the black olives and securely lock on the pressure cooker's lid. Set the cooker to high and cook for 10 minutes.

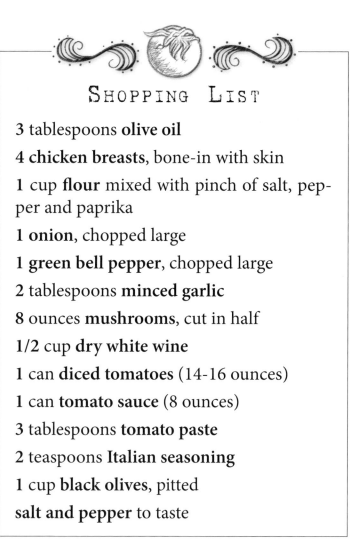

Shopping List

3 tablespoons **olive oil**

4 **chicken breasts**, bone-in with skin

1 cup **flour** mixed with pinch of salt, pepper and paprika

1 **onion**, chopped large

1 **green bell pepper**, chopped large

2 tablespoons **minced garlic**

8 ounces **mushrooms**, cut in half

1/2 cup **dry white wine**

1 can **diced tomatoes** (14-16 ounces)

1 can **tomato sauce** (8 ounces)

3 tablespoons **tomato paste**

2 teaspoons **Italian seasoning**

1 cup **black olives**, pitted

salt and pepper to taste

4. Let the pressure release naturally for 10 minutes before quick releasing the remaining pressure and safely removing lid. Add black olives to the pot and then salt and pepper to taste. Serve over rice or your favorite pasta.

Bob's Tips

Chicken fryer leg quarters can be substituted for the chicken breasts by upping the cooking time to 12 minutes. I like to buy leg quarters in bulk when they're on sale and freeze them for just such recipes.

PREP TIME	COOK TIME	SERVES	TEMPERATURE
5 MINS	10 MINS	SIX	HIGH

PEACHY KEEN CHICKEN

POULTRY

THOUGH THE INGREDIENTS MAY sound like an odd combination, this sweet and savory dish is peachy keen with me! A quick and easy dinner, it's ready faster than you can pick a peach. Unless your kitchen is right under a peach tree that is—if so, you've got me there, but you should really use that peach to make the garnish!

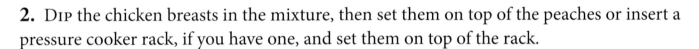

SHOPPING LIST

6 small **boneless, skinless chicken breast halves** (about 2 1/2 pounds)

2 cans **peach slices** (14-16 ounces each can)

2 tablespoons **teriyaki sauce**

1 tablespoon **corn starch**

1. COMBINE peaches and teriyaki sauce in pressure cooker and stir.

2. DIP the chicken breasts in the mixture, then set them on top of the peaches or insert a pressure cooker rack, if you have one, and set them on top of the rack.

3. SECURELY lock on the pressure cooker's lid, set the cooker to high and cook for 10 minutes.

4. PERFORM a quick release to release the cooker's pressure. Safely remove lid, and then remove the chicken breasts and set aside.

5. THICKEN the liquid and cooked peaches into a sauce by combining the corn starch with 2 tablespoons water in a small dish and then stirring it into the cooker on high or brown, with lid off, until thick.

6. RETURN chicken into the sauce to fully coat before serving.

Bob's Tips

I like to boil instant white rice on the stove while the chicken is cooking. It's the perfect accompaniment for the Caribbean and Asian flair of this dish. If you own a grill pan, small indoor grill or panini press; grilling sliced fresh peaches just long enough to mark them makes a most impressive garnish!

POULTRY

Prep Time	Cook Time		Serves	Temperature
10 MINS	4 MINS		SIX	HIGH

Turkey Tetrazzini

Poultry

THIS CREAMY AND VERSATILE NO-BAKE "casserole" recipe is a great one to make when you've got leftover turkey in the fridge. If you don't have any leftover turkey, many stores sell pre-cooked turkey in cubes or strips. Or try making Chicken Tetrazzini with pre-cooked chicken strips or cubes found in any grocery store's refrigerated case. Tuna Tetrazzini can be made by foregoing the turkey and stirring in two well drained cans of tuna fish during the last step of the recipe.

1. ADD egg noodles, chicken base mixed into water, turkey, butter and mushrooms to pressure cooker, securely lock on lid, set the cooker to high and cook for 4 minutes.

SHOPPING LIST

4 cups **egg noodles**, uncooked

3 teaspoons **chicken base** (see page: 12) mixed into 3 cups water

2 cups **cooked turkey**, chopped or cubed

2 tablespoons **butter or margarine**

8 ounces **mushrooms**, sliced

1 cup **shredded Swiss cheese**

1/4 cup **grated Parmesan cheese**

1 cup **sour cream**

3/4 cup **frozen peas**, thawed

1 cup **crackers**, crumbled (Ritz suggested)

salt and pepper to taste

2. PERFORM a quick release to release the cooker's pressure. Safely remove lid and slowly stir in the Swiss cheese, Parmesan cheese, sour cream and peas until cheeses are melted and creamy. Salt and pepper to taste and serve immediately, topped with cracker crumbs.

More traditional Turkey Tetrazzini almost always contains some form of wine. Try adding 1/4 cup of dry sherry during the first step of cooking for something different and delicious; just keep in mind that wine isn't always a hit with younger kids!

Prep Time	Cook Time			Serves	Temperature
10 MINS	8 MINS			FOUR	HIGH

CREAMY CHICKEN CURRY

POULTRY

POULTRY

While "curry" is a generic term for a very broad variety of harmoniously spiced dishes, this recipe with a yogurt sauce is one of the more popular to be served in the Indian restaurants of North America. In the unlikely event that you have leftovers, this dish also makes a great base for chicken salad.

1. Add the vegetable oil to the pressure cooker and heat on high or "brown" with the lid off, until sizzling.

2. Dip chicken breasts in seasoned flour until they are well coated and add to cooker, lightly browning on both sides.

3. Cover with remaining ingredients, except for yogurt and corn starch and securely lock on the pressure cooker's lid. Set the cooker to high and cook for 8 minutes.

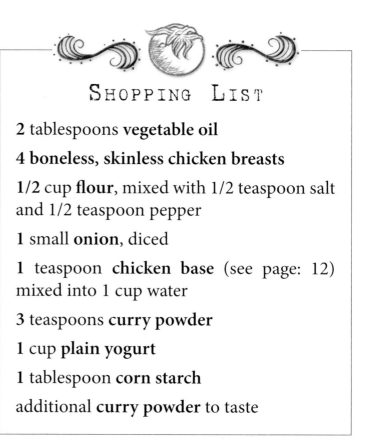

SHOPPING LIST

2 tablespoons **vegetable oil**

4 boneless, skinless chicken breasts

1/2 cup **flour**, mixed with 1/2 teaspoon salt and 1/2 teaspoon pepper

1 small **onion**, diced

1 teaspoon **chicken base** (see page: 12) mixed into 1 cup water

3 teaspoons **curry powder**

1 cup **plain yogurt**

1 tablespoon **corn starch**

additional **curry powder** to taste

4. Let the pressure release naturally for 10 minutes before quick releasing the remaining pressure and safely removing lid.

5. Use tongs to set aside chicken breasts while you make the creamy curry sauce. To make the sauce: set the cooker to high or "brown" with the lid off and wait until cooking liquid is simmering. Thoroughly combine the yogurt and corn starch and then slowly stir into simmering cooking liquid until fully integrated and sauce is creamy and thick. Add any additional curry powder to taste, dip chicken breasts in sauce and serve with additional sauce poured over top.

Bob's Tips

With such a robust flavor, you may want to start with only 2 teaspoons of curry and experiment with different levels, adding in a little at a time until you find the amount that is right for your palate.

Prep Time	Cook Time		Serves	Temperature
15 MINS	10 MINS		FOUR	HIGH

CHICKEN BREAST COQ AU VIN

POULTRY

THE WONDERFULLY RICH FLAVORS OF France all come together in this hearty dish. In fact, it is so French that you may find yourself kissing your fingers and donning a beret. Thankfully, it is not French enough to dress as a mime!

1. ADD the butter, bacon and garlic to the pressure cooker and heat on high or "brown" with the lid off until bacon begins to crisp.

2. DREDGE chicken breasts in seasoned flour until well covered and then add to pressure cooker to lightly brown on both sides.

3. ADD the remaining ingredients, except the corn starch and securely lock on the pressure cooker's lid. Set the cooker to high and cook for 10 minutes.

4. PERFORM a quick release to release the cooker's pressure before safely removing lid. To thicken the sauce: set the pressure cooker to high or "brown" with lid off. Combine the corn starch with 2 tablespoons water in a small dish and stir into the simmering sauce until thick. Salt and pepper to taste and serve with potatoes or over egg noodles, garnished with fresh parsley.

SHOPPING LIST

1 tablespoon **butter or margarine**

2 slices **raw bacon**, cut into 1/4 inch pieces

1 tablespoon **minced garlic**

2-3 pounds **boneless, skinless chicken breasts**

1 cup **flour**, seasoned with a pinch of salt and pepper

2 stalks **celery**, chopped

2 cups **burgundy**

1 teaspoon **beef base** (see page: 12) mixed into 1 cup water

2 tablespoons **tomato paste**

8 ounces **mushrooms**, cleaned and halved

2 cups **white pearl onions**, peeled

1 sprig **fresh thyme** or 1 teaspoon dried

1 **bay leaf**

2 tablespoons **corn starch**

salt and pepper to taste

fresh parsley, for garnish

Bob's Tips

Typically, the herbs in this dish would be prepared into a bouquet garni; a little bundle of the fresh herbs you have on hand, bound together with string for easy retrieval at the end of the cooking process. I use a stainless steel tea steeping ball.

Prep Time	Cook Time		Serves	Temperature
5 MINS	8 MINS		FOUR	HIGH

HONEY DIJON CHICKEN THIGHS

POULTRY

POULTRY

THIS CHICKEN RECIPE IS ONE OF THOSE super fast, super easy and super crowd pleasing family dinners that kids will ask for time and time again. Mix up double the Dijon mustard, honey, brown sugar, salt and pepper and save half for a wonderful dipping sauce!

1. COMBINE all ingredients, except for chicken base in pressure cooker's removable pot (for electronic cookers) or regular pressure cooker pot and stir to evenly coat. Cover and refrigerate for at least 30 minutes to marinate.

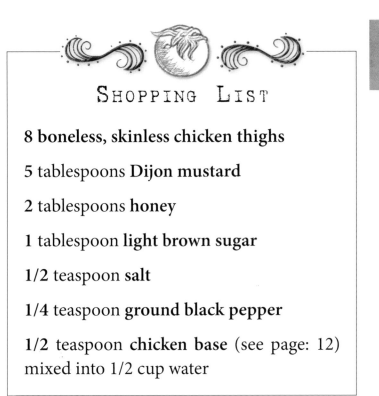

SHOPPING LIST

8 boneless, skinless chicken thighs

5 tablespoons **Dijon mustard**

2 tablespoons **honey**

1 tablespoon **light brown sugar**

1/2 teaspoon **salt**

1/4 teaspoon **ground black pepper**

1/2 teaspoon **chicken base** (see page: 12) mixed into 1/2 cup water

2. ONCE marinated, add the chicken base in water, securely lock on pressure cooker's lid and cook on high for 8 minutes.

3. LET the pressure release naturally for 10 minutes before quick releasing the remaining pressure and safely removing lid. Use tongs to remove thighs and serve alongside rice or your favorite sides.

Bob's Tips

While boneless chicken thighs are more family friendly and easy to eat, bone-in thighs are typically much cheaper, especially when they are on sale and can be substituted without any change in the cooking time. 4 boneless, skinless chicken breasts can also be substituted in a pinch.

Prep Time	Cook Time	Serves	Temperature
10 MINS	10 MINS	SIX	HIGH

CHICKEN MARSALA

POULTRY

YOUR GUESTS WILL BE LOOKING FOR THE Chianti bottle and the red and white checked tablecloth when you serve them this classic Italian entrée. The Marsala wine, which gives the dish its name, combines with mushrooms and chicken to provide a no-fuss, satisfying meal. Accordion music extra.

1. ADD the olive oil and butter to the pressure cooker and heat on high or "brown" with the lid off, until sizzling.

2. DIP chicken breasts in seasoned flour until they are well coated and add to cooker, browning well on both sides.

3. POUR in 1/2 cup of the Marsala wine, chicken base in water and mushrooms.

4. SECURELY lock on the pressure cooker's lid, set the cooker to high and cook for 10 minutes.

SHOPPING LIST

1 tablespoon **olive oil**

2 tablespoons **butter**

6 small **boneless, skinless chicken breast halves** (about 2 pounds)

1/2 cup **flour**, mixed with 1/2 teaspoon salt and 1/2 teaspoon pepper

1 cup **Marsala wine** (or similar dry red) split into two 1/2 cup portions

1 teaspoon **chicken base** (see page: 12) mixed into 1 cup water

16 ounces **mushrooms**, cut in half

2 tablespoons **corn starch**, mixed into 1/4 cup milk

salt and pepper to taste

5. PERFORM a quick release to release the cooker's pressure and safely remove lid.

6. SET the cooker to high or "brown" with lid off and add the remaining 1/2 cup Marsala wine and corn starch mixed with milk. Stir constantly, until the sauce has thickened, then salt and pepper to taste. Serve over your favorite pasta.

Using whole milk or even heavy cream to mix into the corn starch at the end of cooking makes this dish even more decadent. Though white button mushrooms are cheapest and easiest to find, I would highly suggest baby bella mushrooms for their richer flavor.

Prep Time	Cook Time	Serves	Temperature
5 MINS	15 MINS	SIX	HIGH

Turkey Tenderloin with Cranberry Orange Glaze

POULTRY

WITH THIS TURKEY RECIPE, THERE'S NO worrying about whether or not the turkey will fit into a pressure cooker! Turkey tenderloin is arguably the moistest part of the turkey and slices into perfect "medallions" every time.

SHOPPING LIST

1 cup **water**

1/2 cup **orange marmalade**

1 cup **frozen cranberries**

1/4 cup **sugar**

1 **turkey tenderloin**

2 tablespoons **corn starch**

1. COMBINE water, orange marmalade, cranberries and sugar in pressure cooker and stir.

2. PLACE turkey tenderloin over top mixture in cooker and then securely lock on the pressure cooker's lid. Set the cooker to high and cook for 15 minutes.

3. PERFORM a quick release to release the cooker's pressure. Safely remove lid, and then remove the tenderloin, setting aside to rest under tin foil.

4. THICKEN the glaze by combining the corn starch with 2 tablespoons water in a small dish and then stirring it into the cooker on high or "brown", with lid off, simmering until thick.

5. CARVE turkey loin and serve drizzled with glaze.

Many stores only carry turkey tenderloins pre-marinated in a range of different flavors. This isn't necessarily a bad thing as lemon pepper marinated turkey tenderloin goes quite well in the glaze.

Prep Time	Cook Time	Serves	Temperature
10 MINS	8 MINS	FOUR	HIGH

Paprika Chicken in Sour Cream Gravy

Poultry

THIS Hungarian dish is an exciting way to spruce up dinner with ease. It's seemingly exotic while utilizing everyday ingredients that you may already have in the cupboard! So get cooking!

1. ADD the butter to the pressure cooker and heat on high or "brown" with the lid off, until sizzling.

2. COMBINE seasoned flour with paprika and dip chicken breasts in this mixture until they are well coated. Add coated breasts to cooker, lightly browning on both sides before adding onion and garlic to cooker and sautéing for 2-3 minutes more.

3. COVER with remaining ingredients, except for sour cream and corn starch and securely lock on the pressure cooker's lid. Set the cooker to high and cook for 8 minutes.

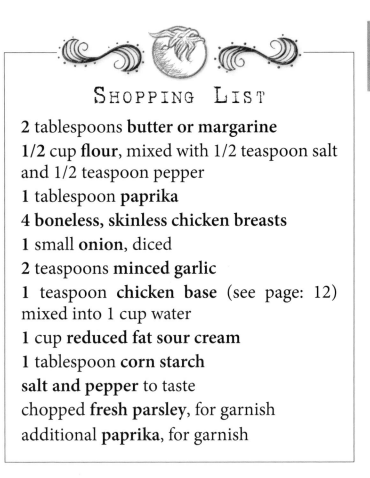

SHOPPING LIST

2 tablespoons **butter or margarine**

1/2 cup **flour**, mixed with 1/2 teaspoon salt and 1/2 teaspoon pepper

1 tablespoon **paprika**

4 boneless, skinless chicken breasts

1 small **onion**, diced

2 teaspoons **minced garlic**

1 teaspoon **chicken base** (see page: 12) mixed into 1 cup water

1 cup **reduced fat sour cream**

1 tablespoon **corn starch**

salt and pepper to taste

chopped **fresh parsley**, for garnish

additional **paprika**, for garnish

4. LET the pressure release naturally for 10 minutes before quick releasing the remaining pressure and safely removing lid.

5. USE tongs to set aside chicken breasts while you make the sauce. To make the sauce: set the cooker to high or "brown" with the lid off and wait until cooking liquid is simmering. Thoroughly combine the sour cream and corn starch and then slowly stir into simmering cooking liquid until fully integrated and sauce is creamy and thick. Salt and pepper to taste, dip chicken breasts in sauce and serve topped with chopped parsley and a pinch of paprika.

Bob's Tips

I've heard that Hungarian or sweet paprika works best in this recipe if your local store stocks it, but regular paprika has worked just fine for me.

POULTRY

Prep Time	Cook Time	Serves	Temperature
5 MINS	10 MINS	SIX	HIGH

Teriyaki Chicken Wings

POULTRY

These Asian style chicken wings are exploding with so much marinated flavor that you serve them "naked"— without all the sticky, gooey mess of most typical chicken wing sauces. With the deep taste of teriyaki and sesame, get ready to take your next party to a whole different continent!

1. Combine all ingredients, except 2 tablespoons sesame oil and the toasted sesame seeds, in a large bowl and cover with plastic wrap. Refrigerate for at least two hours (overnight recommended) to marinate.

2. Heat 2 tablespoons sesame oil in pressure cooker on high or "brown" with lid off until sizzling.

Shopping List

2 pounds **chicken wings**, drum and wings separated

6 tablespoons **sesame oil** (4 tablespoons for marinade and 2 to brown)

1 cup **low sodium teriyaki sauce**

1 tablespoon **lemon juice**

2 tablespoons **sugar**

1/2 teaspoon **crushed red pepper**, optional

toasted sesame seeds, for garnish

3. Using tongs, remove chicken wings from marinade (reserving marinade) and place in cooker to brown. Stir around, lightly browning as many of the wings on as many sides as possible.

4. Pour marinade over browned wings, securely lock on the pressure cooker's lid and cook on high for 7 minutes.

5. Let the pressure release naturally for 10 minutes before quick releasing any remaining pressure to safely remove lid. Remove with tongs and serve topped with toasted sesame seeds.

 To toast raw sesame seeds: heat them in a pan on the stove over medium heat until golden brown, about 4 minutes. Be sure to shake the pan constantly to keep them moving.

Cooking Times
Pork and Ham

When cooking pork roasts, browning the meat first is recommended. Let the pressure release naturally for 10 minutes for more tender meat. If hams are too large to fit into your cooker, they can be carefully cut off the bone in large sections before cooking (lower the cooking time to 30 minutes).

Pork	Size	Liquid	Cook Minutes	Temp
Baby Back Ribs	2-4 pounds	1 cup	20	high
Chops	1/2 inch thick	1/2 cup	7	high
Chops	1 inch thick	1/2 cup	15	high
Loin	3-5 pounds	2 cups	50	high
Roasts	3-5 pounds	2 cups	45	high
Sausages, raw	1-3 pounds	covered	10	high
Spareribs	2-4 pounds	1 cup	10	high
Ham				
Hocks	any	covered	60	high
Steaks	4 steaks	1 cup	8	high
Whole, cooked	4-6 pounds	3 cups	40	high

PORK AND HAM

Prep Time	Cook Time		Serves	Temperature
5 Mins	40 Mins		Six	High

Two Can Cola Pork Roast

Pork and Ham

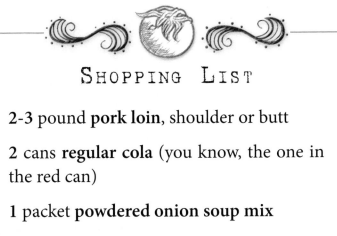

THIS SPECTACULAR PORK ROAST RECIPE IS by far the greatest mystery in this book. Just how can cola make gravy that is this good? I'm not sure that even I know the answer, but I do know that it's delicious and definitely not as sweet as you would think it to be.

Shopping List

2-3 pound **pork loin**, shoulder or butt

2 cans **regular cola** (you know, the one in the red can)

1 packet **powdered onion soup mix**

2 tablespoons **corn starch**

PORK

1. **P**LACE the roast and all ingredients except corn starch into pressure cooker and securely lock on the lid. Set the cooker to high and cook for 40 minutes.

2. **L**ET the pressure release naturally for 10 minutes before quick releasing any remaining pressure and safely removing lid.

3. **C**HECK roast for tenderness. If not fork tender, re-secure the lid and cook on high an additional ten minutes, with a 10 minute natural release.

4. **R**EMOVE roast to rest under tin foil as you thicken the gravy. To thicken gravy: set the cooker to high or "brown" with lid off until cooking juices are simmering. Mix corn starch with 2 tablespoons water and slowly add to simmering juices, stirring constantly, until thick.

5. **C**ARVE roast and serve with plenty of gravy.

I like a good pork roast with mashed potatoes and fresh green beans, but if you'd like to make this into a one pot meal, throw in your favorite vegetables when you remove the roast to rest. 5 minutes under high pressure is a pretty safe amount of time for quartered potatoes and large chunked carrots or celery.

Prep Time	Cook Time		Serves	Temperature
10 MINS	15 MINS		SIX	HIGH

PORK VINDALOO

PORK AND HAM

DUST OFF YOUR ADVENTUROUS STREAK for this traditional Indian curry dish that is plentifully spiced and ready to take your taste buds for a ride! While Vindaloo has a reputation for being HOT, don't let that scare you off as this recipe is a relatively mild variation.

1. COMBINE all ingredients, except for chicken base in pressure cooker's removable pot (for electronic cookers) or regular pressure cooker pot and stir to evenly coat. Cover and refrigerate for at least 2 hours to marinate.

2. ONCE marinated, add the chicken base in water, securely lock on pressure cooker's lid and cook on high for 15 minutes.

3. LET the pressure release naturally for 10 minutes before quick releasing the remaining pressure and safely removing lid. Salt and pepper to taste and serve over rice.

SHOPPING LIST

2 pounds boneless **pork loin**, cut into 1 inch cubes

1 **onion**, diced

2 tablespoon **olive oil**

1 tablespoon **minced garlic**

1/4 cup **red wine vinegar**

1 teaspoon **ground dry mustard**

1/2 teaspoon **cumin**

1/2 teaspoon **ground cloves**

1/4 teaspoon **chili powder**

1/2 teaspoon **ground cinnamon**

1/2 teaspoon **ground cardamom**

1 teaspoon **ground turmeric**

1/2 teaspoon **ground ginger**

1 teaspoon **sugar**

1 teaspoon **chicken base** (see page: 12) mixed into 1 cup water

salt and pepper to taste

If your spice rack isn't full to the hilt, you can substitute 3 teaspoons of curry powder in place of all of the spice ingredients except for the cinnamon in this recipe.

PREP TIME	COOK TIME		SERVES	TEMPERATURE
15 MINS	14 MINS		FOUR	HIGH

PORK LOIN CHOPS WITH APPLE AND SHERRY

PORK AND HAM

IT'S NO SECRET THAT PORK AND APPLE are meant to be together. In this recipe the juicy, boneless pork loin chops cook surrounded by thick cut apples, sherry, cinnamon and a little touch of brown sugar for a sweet note that's delicious but not overwhelming. Serve this in the fall when apples are at their peak.

1. ADD the oil to the pressure cooker and heat on high or "brown" with the lid off until sizzling.

2. ADD pork chops and onion and sauté until chops are lightly browned on both sides.

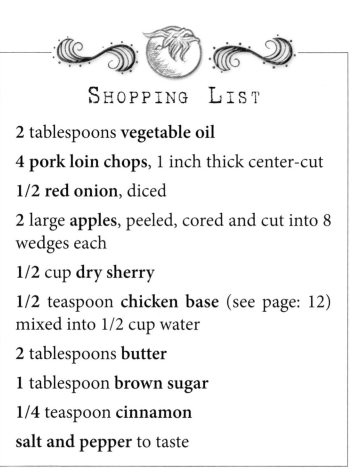

SHOPPING LIST

2 tablespoons **vegetable oil**

4 **pork loin chops**, 1 inch thick center-cut

1/2 **red onion**, diced

2 large **apples**, peeled, cored and cut into 8 wedges each

1/2 cup **dry sherry**

1/2 teaspoon **chicken base** (see page: 12) mixed into 1/2 cup water

2 tablespoons **butter**

1 tablespoon **brown sugar**

1/4 teaspoon **cinnamon**

salt and pepper to taste

3. COVER with the remaining ingredients, securely lock on the pressure cooker's lid, set the cooker to high and cook for 14 minutes.

4. PERFORM a quick release to release the cooker's pressure. Safely remove lid, salt and pepper to taste and serve drizzled with cooking liquid.

Bob's Tips

Any cut of pork chop will work well in this recipe, boneless or bone-in. You can even save money by buying the entire pork loin and cutting the chops off yourself, freezing the rest of the loin for future meals!

PREP TIME	COOK TIME	SERVES	TEMPERATURE
10 MINS	90 MINS	TEN	HIGH

PULLED PORK SANDWICHES

PORK AND HAM

PORK

A PULLED PORK SANDWICH MAY SEEM LIKE such a simple picnic indulgence, but preparing one the traditional way would require a smoker an entire day of it fired up. With the pressure cooker bringing the cooking time down from 8 hours to 90 minutes, you can actually have your picnic lunch in time… for lunch.

1. COMBINE all Dry Rub ingredients in a small bowl.

2. CUT pork into 2 inch thick pieces (to speed up cooking time) then cut 1/8 inch deep, crisscrossing grooves into the pieces. Coat pieces with Dry Rub, pushing it into the grooves. Let sit for five minutes.

3. ADD the chicken base in water and liquid smoke to the pressure cooker. Place the pork pieces over top as separated from each other as possible.

4. POUR BBQ Sauce over top pork pieces and securely lock on the pressure cooker's lid. Set the cooker to high and cook for 90 minutes.

5. LET the pressure release naturally for at least 10 minutes before quick releasing any remaining pressure and safely removing lid. Pork should be fork tender and shred easily. If not, re-secure the lid and cook an additional 20 minutes on high.

6. SERVE pulled apart on sesame seed buns with your favorite toppings. Sandwiches pictured at left are made my favorite way, with sliced red onion and cheddar cheese.

SHOPPING LIST

Dry Rub

4-5 pound **pork shoulder or butt**

1 tablespoon **chili powder**

2 teaspoons **ground cumin**

1/2 teaspoon **ground allspice**

2 teaspoons **salt**

1 teaspoon **ground black pepper**

Pulled Pork

4-5 pound **pork shoulder or butt**

1 teaspoon **chicken base** (see page: 12) mixed into 1 cup water

1 teaspoon **liquid smoke**

1 batch **Stick to Your Ribs BBQ Sauce**, recipe page: 187

Sandwiches

sesame seed buns

sliced **red onion**, optional

cheddar cheese slices, optional

Bob's Tips More traditional pulled pork sandwiches are topped directly with coleslaw and I can tell you that it's delicious! My Stick to Your Ribs BBQ Sauce is extra thick to withstand the extra liquid of pressure cooking, but you can use a bottle of your favorite sauce and 4 tablespoons tomato paste in it's place.

PREP TIME	COOK TIME	SERVES	TEMPERATURE
10 MINS	20 MINS	SIX	HIGH

BABY BACK RIBS

PORK AND HAM

NOTHING SAYS COMFORT QUITE LIKE this flavorful dish. The combination of tangy barbecue sauce and tender meat will satisfy the heartiest of appetites. Pair them with coleslaw and corn on the cob and you'll have a picnic lunch. Pair them with mashed potatoes and green beans and you have a full-fledged country supper.

SHOPPING LIST

1/2 cup **water**

3 pounds **baby back pork ribs**

1 batch **Stick to Your Ribs BBQ Sauce**, recipe page: 187

1. ADD water to pressure cooker.

2. CUT ribs into sections small enough to fit into pressure cooker and generously coat with the BBQ sauce. Lean ribs against the sides, standing upright in the cooker.

3. ADD any remaining BBQ sauce to water at bottom of cooker, securely lock on the pressure cooker's lid and cook on high for 20 minutes.

4. PERFORM a quick release to release the cooker's pressure. Safely remove lid and serve.

 To give the ribs a little more color (and flavor) place cooked ribs on a sheet pan under the broiler for a few minutes until the sugars in the sauce begin to char. My Stick to Your Ribs BBQ Sauce is extra thick to withstand the extra liquid of pressure cooking, but you can use a bottle of your favorite sauce and 4 tablespoons tomato paste in its place for the same spectacular results.

PREP TIME	COOK TIME		SERVES	TEMPERATURE
5 MINS	40 MINS		EIGHT	HIGH

MOJO MARINATED PORK ROAST

PORK AND HAM

PORK

T HIS ISLAND SPICED PORK ROAST GETS ALL of it's amazing citrus, garlic and fresh herb flavors from a marinade called Mojo Criollo, which you can find in the marinades section (usually near the condiments) of your local grocery store. If you are still having trouble finding it, check the ethnic aisle of your store and you should be in luck!

1. MARINATE roast in the mojo criollo marinade, covered and refrigerated for at least 2 hours before preparing to cook.

SHOPPING LIST

2-4 pound **pork roast**

1 bottle **mojo criollo marinade** (minimum 12 ounces)

2 tablespoons **vegetable oil**

1/2 teaspoon **chicken base** (see page: 12) mixed into 1/2 cup water

---

2. ADD the oil to the pressure cooker and heat on high or "brown" with the lid off until sizzling.

3. REMOVE roast from and reserve the marinade. Place roast in cooker and brown on both top and bottom.

4. POUR in chicken base mixed in water and the reserved marinade and securely lock on the pressure cooker's lid. Set the cooker to high and cook for 40 minutes.

5. LET the pressure release naturally for 10 minutes before quick releasing any remaining pressure and safely removing lid. Roast should be fork tender. If not, re-lock on lid and cook on high an additional 10 minutes. Remove roast and let rest under tin foil for 5 minutes before carving. Traditionally, the roast is shredded into large chunks by fork, not sliced. Serve drizzled with cooking liquid to keep moist.

Though the roast will taste best when browned, you can make this recipe even easier by marinating the roast straight in the pressure cooker pot before skipping all the way to step 4 to cook. You'll create less dishes and get dinner to the table even faster!

Prep Time	Cook Time		Serves	Temperature
5 MINS	5 MINS		FOUR	HIGH

Ham Steaks with Pineapple Cherry Glaze

Pork and Ham

You don't need to spend all day baking a ham to have a delicious glazed ham dinner. This recipe is as simple and quick as it gets, with a sweet and tangy glaze made all the better by the ham's natural juices released into it as it cooks under pressure.

1. ADD the juice of 1 can pineapple rings and 1 jar maraschino cherries to the pressure cooker, setting aside the rings and cherries for later. Add brown sugar and water and stir.

2. FOR best results, place a metal rack over liquid and set ham steaks on top of rack. Securely lock on the pressure cooker's lid, set the cooker to high and cook for 5 minutes.

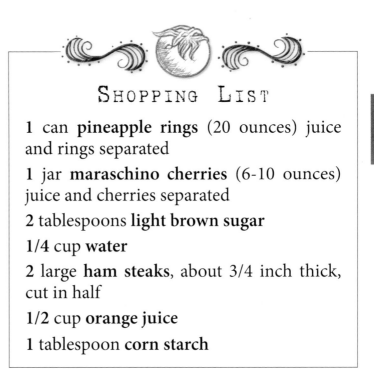

Shopping List

1 can **pineapple rings** (20 ounces) juice and rings separated

1 jar **maraschino cherries** (6-10 ounces) juice and cherries separated

2 tablespoons **light brown sugar**

1/4 cup **water**

2 large **ham steaks**, about 3/4 inch thick, cut in half

1/2 cup **orange juice**

1 tablespoon **corn starch**

PORK

3. LET the pressure release naturally for 5 minutes before quick releasing the remaining pressure and safely removing lid. Set aside ham steaks to rest under tin foil and carefully remove metal rack with tongs.

4. SWITCH cooker to high or "brown" with lid off until liquid is simmering. Mix orange juice and corn starch in a small bowl until well combined, then slowly stir into simmering liquid in cooker to thicken and create the glaze.

5. ADD pineapple rings and cherries to the glaze to warm up and then serve over ham steaks with your favorite sides.

Bob's Tips

For the best presentation, serve each ham steak with one or two pineapple rings, maraschino cherries sitting in the center of the rings. When shopping, ham steaks with the bone-in retain all of the texture of a full baked ham, while boneless ham steaks tend to have more in common with luncheon meat than a true baked ham.

PREP TIME	COOK TIME	SERVES	TEMPERATURE
10 MINS	40 MINS	SIX	HIGH

PORK LOIN WITH MILK GRAVY

PORK AND HAM

PORK

WHILE THE IDEA OF SIMMERING A PORK loin in milk may sound strange, it really highlights the wonderful flavors of the meat itself. In fact, the flavors it brings out are so wonderful that a tiny pinch of rosemary is the only herb in the dish!

1. ADD the butter, oil and pork loin to the pressure cooker and heat on high or "brown" with the lid off until loin is lightly browned on all sides.

2. COVER with remaining ingredients, except milk and corn starch into pressure cooker and securely lock on the lid. Set the cooker to high and cook for 40 minutes.

SHOPPING LIST

2 tablespoons **butter**

1 tablespoon **vegetable oil**

2-3 pound **pork loin**

1 tablespoon **minced garlic**

1 cup **dry white wine**

1 teaspoon **chicken base** (see page: 12) mixed into 1 cup water

1/4 teaspoon **dried rosemary**

1 cup **whole milk**

2 tablespoons **corn starch**

salt and pepper to taste

3. LET the pressure release naturally for 10 minutes before quick releasing any remaining pressure and safely removing lid.

4. ADD milk and set the cooker to high or "brown", with lid off. Simmer for 10 minutes.

5. REMOVE roast to rest under tin foil as you thicken the gravy. To thicken gravy: mix corn starch with 2 tablespoons water and slowly add to simmering juices, stirring constantly, until thick. Salt and pepper gravy to taste.

6. CARVE roast and serve with plenty of gravy.

Bob's Tips The longer you simmer the pork in the milk after cooking under pressure, the better the gravy will turn out.

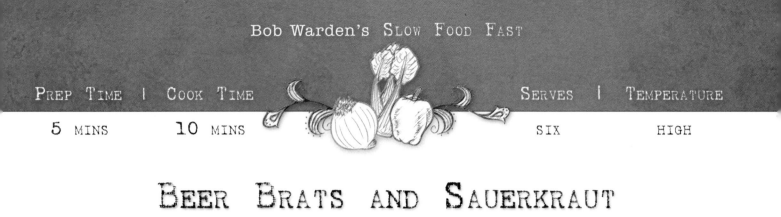

Prep Time	Cook Time	Serves	Temperature
5 MINS	10 MINS	SIX	HIGH

Beer Brats and Sauerkraut

Pork and Ham

You don't have to be from Wisconsin to enjoy this traditional German take on the hot dog. A common staple of tailgate parties, this dish can help get a football fan through that long stretch between the NFL draft and the start of football season. Just make sure you have plenty of hot mustard on hand and save some of the beer to drink with the brats.

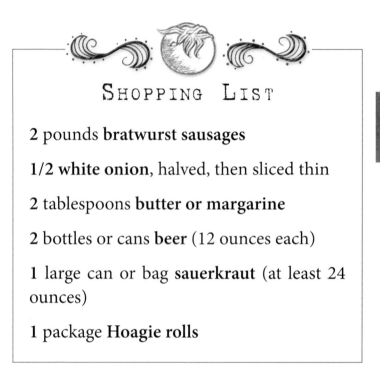

Shopping List

2 pounds **bratwurst sausages**

1/2 **white onion**, halved, then sliced thin

2 tablespoons **butter or margarine**

2 bottles or cans **beer** (12 ounces each)

1 large can or bag **sauerkraut** (at least 24 ounces)

1 package **Hoagie rolls**

PORK

1. ADD bratwurst, onion, butter, beer and 1/3 of the sauerkraut to the pressure cooker.

2. SECURELY lock on the pressure cooker's lid, set the cooker to high and cook for 10 minutes.

3. PERFORM a quick release to release the cooker's pressure. Safely remove lid and stir in remaining sauerkraut. Serve with a slotted spoon into Hoagie rolls.

Bob's Tips The water in the onions and sauerkraut has a tendency to dilute the beer, so while a lager is more typical of beer brats, I say that the darker the beer the better! Guinness Irish Stout is as dark as coffee and will most certainly give you the most bang for your buck!

Prep Time	Cook Time		Serves	Temperature
10 MINS	10 MINS		SIX	HIGH

PORK SOUVLAKI

PORK AND HAM

Though Souvlaki kebabs are usually grilled, this recipe has all of the traditional flavors of oregano, olive oil, garlic and lemon in less time than you can preheat a grill! Warm some pita bread in a 300 degree oven while the Souvlaki is cooking and put it all together with my Tzatziki Sauce and it may be something new (unless you've been to any diner in New England!), but I guarantee that you'll be back for seconds!

1. Combine all ingredients, except for chicken base, skewers, pita bread and Tzatziki sauce in pressure cooker's removable pot (for electronic cookers) or regular pressure cooker pot and stir to evenly coat. Cover and refrigerate for at least 2 hours to marinate.

2. Once marinated, add the chicken base in water, securely lock on pressure cooker's lid and cook on high for 10 minutes.

SHOPPING LIST

1 1/2 pounds **boneless pork loin**, cut into 1 inch cubes

3 tablespoons **olive oil**

1/4 cup **lemon juice**

1 tablespoon **minced garlic**

2 tablespoons **dried oregano**

1/4 teaspoon **salt**

1/4 teaspoon **ground black pepper**

1/2 teaspoon **chicken base** (see page: 12) mixed into 1/2 cup water

bamboo skewers, optional

pita bread, optional

Tzatziki Sauce, recipe page: 182

3. Let the pressure release naturally for 10 minutes before quick releasing the remaining pressure and safely removing lid. Use tongs or a slotted spoon to remove pork from liquid. Let cool for 2-3 minutes before threading pork onto bamboo skewers and serving with warm pita bread and Tzatziki Sauce.

Another typical way of eating Souvlaki is right on the pita, topped with a generous amount of Tzatziki sauce, fresh sliced tomatoes and red onion. It is also commonly served over rice pilaf. In New England diners, you're sure to get a small Greek salad on the side.

PORK

Prep Time	Cook Time	Serves	Temperature
15 MINS	45 MINS	SIX	HIGH

PORK POT ROAST

PORK AND HAM

THIS CLASSIC FAMILY MEAL IS LIKE TWO recipes in one. The first is the pot roast dinner and the second is the sliced pork or Cuban sandwich made from the leftovers the next day!

1. ADD the oil to the pressure cooker and heat on high or "brown" with the lid off until sizzling. Brown the seasoned roast well on all sides.

2. ADD remaining "Roast" ingredients to pressure cooker and securely lock on the lid. Set the cooker to high and cook for 40 minutes.

3. LET the pressure release naturally for 10 minutes before quick releasing any remaining pressure and safely removing lid.

4. ADD all Vegetable ingredients, except the corn starch and re-lock on the pressure cooker's lid. Set the cooker to high and cook for an additional 5 minutes.

5. PERFORM a quick release to release the cooker's pressure. Safely remove lid and set aside roast to rest under tin foil as you thicken the gravy. To thicken gravy: set the cooker to high or "brown" with lid off until cooking juices and vegetables are simmering. Mix corn starch with 2 tablespoons water and slowly add to simmering juice, stirring constantly, until thick. Carve roast and serve with vegetables and gravy.

SHOPPING LIST

Roast
4 tablespoons **vegetable oil**
2-3 pound **pork loin**, shoulder or butt, seasoned with 1/2 teaspoon salt and pepper
1/2 cup **dry white wine**
2 teaspoons **chicken base** (see page: 12) mixed into 2 cups water
2 tablespoons **minced garlic**
1 sprig **fresh thyme**, or 1 teaspoon dried
2 **bay leaves**

Vegetables
6 small **redskin potatoes**, halved
2 small **onions**, peeled and quartered
1 cup **baby carrots**
2 stalks **celery**, cut into 1 inch pieces
2 tablespoons **corn starch**
salt and pepper to taste

Bob's Tips This recipe, without the vegetables is a must for a good homemade Cuban sandwich with sliced pork, ham, Swiss cheese, pickles and mustard. Sliced pork lunchmeat is hard to come by in grocery stores and if you can find it, its texture usually bears more resemblance to bologna than pork.

Prep Time	Cook Time		Serves	Temperature
10 mins	10 mins		six	high

Sweet and Sour Spareribs

Pork and Ham

Spareribs are a Chinese Restaurant favorite of mine but at only 3 or 4 ribs to an order, assembling enough of them for a party would cost an arm and a rib! These have all the tangy and sweet components to recreate my favorite at a fraction of the price.

1. Add ribs to pressure cooker and then combine all other ingredients in a mixing bowl, mixing well.

2. Pour the sauce mixture over top ribs. Securely lock on the pressure cooker's lid, set the cooker to high and cook for 10 minutes.

Shopping List

2-4 pounds **spareribs**, cut into 4 rib pieces

1/2 **onion**, diced

3/4 cup **water**

2/3 cup **light brown sugar**

1 cup **ketchup**

2 tablespoons **vinegar**

2 tablespoons **orange juice**

2 tablespoons **soy sauce**

PORK

3. Let the pressure release naturally for 10 minutes before (carefully!) quick releasing the remaining pressure and safely removing lid. Serve as an appetizer or serve with rice.

Bob's Tips

Sweet and sour not your thing? Make BBQ Spareribs by replacing everything but the ribs and water with a batch of my Stick to Your Ribs BBQ sauce, recipe page: 187.

Prep Time	Cook Time		Serves	Temperature
15 MINS	10 MINS		SIX	HIGH

Italian Sausage, Peppers and Onion Hoagies

PORK AND HAM

Hoagie, Hero, Grinder or whatever you'd like to call it, this recipe for Italian sausage, peppers and onions will make your next sandwich worthy of a name with gusto! Though the recipe calls for sweet Italian sausage, try it with hot Italian sausage if you dare. Cook those up on game day for a touchdown every time!

1. Add the oil to the pressure cooker and heat on high or "brown" with the lid off.

2. Add sausages and sauté until well browned on two sides.

3. Add the garlic and about 1/4 of the onions and sauté together for another minute.

4. Add the remaining ingredients, securely lock on the pressure cooker's lid, set the cooker to high and cook for 10 minutes.

Shopping List

2 tablespoons **olive oil**

2 pounds **sweet or mild Italian sausage**

2 teaspoons **minced garlic**

2 **white onions**, peeled, cut in half and sliced in 1/2 inch wide strips

1 cup **green bell pepper**, cored and sliced in 1/2 inch wide strips

1 cup **red bell pepper**, cored and sliced in 1/2 inch wide strips

1/2 cup **dry white wine**

1 cup **water**

1 teaspoon **Italian seasoning**

1/2 teaspoon **salt**

1/2 teaspoon **ground black pepper**

6 **Hoagie rolls**

Parmesan cheese, for garnish

5. Perform a quick release to release the cooker's pressure. Safely remove lid and serve with a slotted spoon into Hoagie rolls. Top with a generous amount of grated Parmesan cheese.

Though nothing beats an Italian sausage Hoagie, you can also serve the sausage, peppers and onions over pasta with red sauce or even alongside roasted potatoes and veggies.

PORK

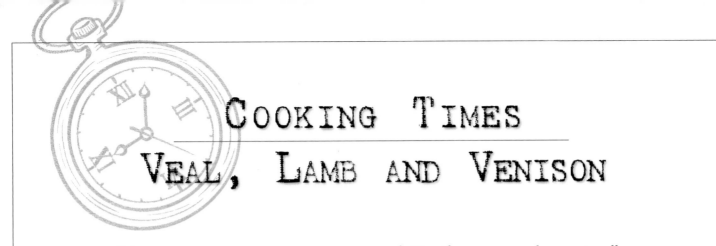

COOKING TIMES
VEAL, LAMB AND VENISON

WHEN COOKING VEAL, LAMB AND VENISON, letting the pressure release naturally for 10 minutes is recommended for the most tender meat. However, quick releasing the pressure is recommended for thin cuts of veal. Brown the meat before pressure cooking for best flavor.

VEAL	SIZE	LIQUID	COOK MINUTES	TEMP
ROAST	3-4 pounds	2 cups	45	high
SHANKS	2 inch thick	1 1/2 cups	20	high
STEAKS	1/2 inch thick	1/2 cup	5	high
LAMB				
BREAST	2-3 pounds	2 cups	40	high
CHOPS	1/2 inch thick	1/2 cup	5	high
CHOPS	1 inch thick	1/2 cup	12	high
LEG	3-4 pounds	2 cups	40	high
SHANKS	cut in half	1 1/2 cups	25	high
VENISON				
ROAST	4-5 pounds	2 cups	40	high
STEW MEAT	1 inch cubes	1 1/2 cups	12	high

VEAL AND LAMB

Prep Time	Cook Time		Serves	Temperature
15 MINS	25 MINS		SIX	HIGH

Braised Lamb Shanks with Lemon and Mint

Veal and Lamb

EVEN IF YOU HAIL FROM THE HEART OF Scandinavia, you'll be saying "Opa!" when you taste this delicious, traditional Greek pairing of flavors. The sharpness of the lemon and the fresh taste of the mint are perfect compliments to the unique flavor of the lamb.

1. HEAT the oil in the pressure cooker on high or "brown" with the lid off until sizzling.

2. ADD the lamb shanks and brown well on all sides. When almost browned, add garlic to infuse it into the meat.

3. ADD wine, chicken base mixed with water, tomato paste, sliced lemon and fresh mint and securely lock on the pressure cooker's lid. Set the cooker to high and cook for 20 minutes.

4. PERFORM a quick release to release the cooker's pressure before safely removing lid. Add onion, carrots and celery and re-secure the cooker's lid. Set the cooker to high and cook an additional 5 minutes.

SHOPPING LIST

2 tablespoons **vegetable oil**

3 **lamb shanks**, cut in half, excess fat trimmed off

1 tablespoon **minced garlic**

1 cup **dry white wine**

2 teaspoons **chicken base** (see page: 12) mixed into 2 cups water

3 tablespoons **tomato paste**

1 **lemon**, sliced thick

1 tablespoon **fresh mint**, chopped

1 **onion**, sliced thick

2 **carrots**, cut into 2 inch lengths

2 stalks **celery**, cut into 2 inch lengths

salt and pepper to taste

zest of **1 lemon**, to top

fresh mint, chopped, to top

5. LET the pressure release naturally for 10 minutes before quick releasing the remaining pressure and safely removing lid. Salt and pepper to taste. Serve topped with lemon zest and fresh chopped mint.

Bob's Tips Make sure to ask your butcher to cut the lamb shanks in half; do not attempt to do it yourself! Lamb shoulder can also be used in place of the shanks by cutting the shoulder into 2 inch thick pieces.

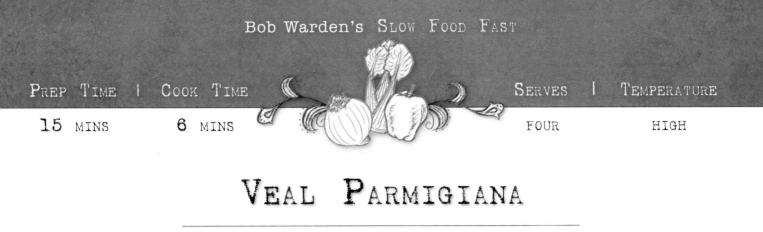

Prep Time	Cook Time		Serves	Temperature
15 MINS	6 MINS		FOUR	HIGH

VEAL PARMIGIANA

VEAL AND LAMB

This classic Italian dish is not as crispy in the pressure cooker, but it's so easy and so tender that I absolutely had to include it here. Plus, if veal isn't your thing, this is like two recipes in one as thin chicken breasts are easily substituted!

1. DIP veal scallopini in bread crumbs until they are well coated.

2. POUR the olive oil into the pressure cooker and heat on high or "brown" with the lid off, until sizzling.

SHOPPING LIST

1-2 pounds **veal scallopini** (about 1/4 inch thick)

1 cup **Italian bread crumbs**

2 tablespoons **olive oil**

1 jar store bought **marinara sauce** (24-26 ounces)

1/2 cup **dry red wine**

1/2 cup **Parmesan cheese**

1 cup **mozzarella cheese**, optional

3. ADD veal to pressure cooker, browning each piece on both sides before adding in remaining ingredients, except for Parmesan and mozzarella cheese.

4. SECURELY lock on the pressure cooker's lid, set the cooker to high and cook for 6 minutes.

5. LET the pressure release naturally for 5 minutes before quick releasing the remaining pressure and safely removing lid.

6. IMMEDIATELY top with Parmesan and mozzarella cheeses and gently set lid on top of cooker (no need to lock on or secure) to keep in some heat and melt the cheese. Once cheese has melted, serve with some of the sauce over pasta.

Bob's Tips If you would like to brown the cheese, skip the last step in the recipe and instead top veal with cheese on a sheet pan. Place under your oven's broiler on high and watch carefully as the cheese will brown VERY fast!

Prep Time	Cook Time		Serves	Temperature
15 MINS	20 MINS		FOUR	HIGH

Osso Buco

Veal and Lamb

THE POSTER CHILD OF THE PRESSURE cooker, Osso Buco is a typically time consuming and labor intensive dish of braised veal shanks that most people would never attempt to make at home. With only a 20 minute cook time, the pressure cooker changes things so dramatically, you may not even have enough time to make the gremolata—a lemon and herb topping that adds another dimension of flavor to an already extraordinary dish.

1. ADD the olive oil to the pressure cooker and heat on high or "brown" with the lid off.

2. DIP veal shanks in seasoned flour until they are well coated and add to cooker to lightly brown on both sides.

3. ADD the garlic, onion, carrots and celery and sauté for 1 minute before covering with remaining Osso Buco ingredients.

4. SECURELY lock on the pressure cooker's lid, set the cooker to high and cook for 20 minutes.

5. WHILE the Osso Buco is cooking, make the Gremolata by combining all Gremolata ingredients in a small bowl.

SHOPPING LIST

Osso Buco
3 tablespoons **olive oil**
3-4 pounds **veal shanks**, 4 shanks cut 1 to 1 1/2 inch thick
1 cup **flour**, mixed with 1/2 teaspoon salt and 1/2 teaspoon pepper
1 **red onion**, chopped
2 tablespoons **minced garlic**
2 **carrots**, cut into 1/4 inch discs
2 stalks **celery**, chopped
1 teaspoon **chicken base** (see page: 12) mixed into 1/2 cup water
1 cup **white wine**
1 can **diced tomatoes** (14-16 ounces)
2 tablespoons **tomato paste**
2 teaspoons **Italian seasoning**
salt and pepper to taste

Gremolata
1 tablespoon **minced garlic**
1/2 cup **fresh parsley**, chopped
zest of **1 lemon**
1/4 teaspoon **salt**

6. WHEN the Osso Buco is finished cooking, let the pressure release naturally for 10 minutes before quick releasing the remaining pressure and safely removing lid. Salt and pepper to taste. Serve topped with Gremolata.

Serve over your favorite risotto for the true Italian presentation. Osso Buco is one of the few dishes Italians don't serve the meat and starch as separate courses!

VEAL/LAMB

Prep Time	Cook Time		Serves	Temperature
15 MINS	5 MINS		SIX	HIGH

Olive Infused Lamb Chops with Red Wine

Veal and Lamb

This dish shouts out sunshine. With very little effort you can picture yourself sitting on a terrace overlooking the Mediterranean, sharing a meal with friends. Have a glass of wine while you're cooking and enjoy the feel of the sun on your face.

1. Combine all ingredients, except lamb chops, in a blender or food processor and blend until smooth to make a marinade.

2. Cover lamb chops with marinade in a large bowl or food storage container. Cover and refrigerate for at least 1 hour before cooking.

Shopping List

2 tablespoons **olive oil**

1/4 cup **black olives**, pitted

2 tablespoons **minced garlic**

1 teaspoon **dried rosemary**

1 teaspoon **dried oregano**

1 cup **dry red wine**

6 **lamb chops**, 1/2 inch thick, trimmed of excess fat

3. Heat the pressure cooker on high or "brown" with the lid off and add 2 tablespoons of marinade to pot.

4. Add the lamb chops to cooker and lightly brown on both sides for about 2-3 minutes.

5. Cover chops with remaining marinade and securely lock on the pressure cooker's lid. Set the cooker to high and cook for 5 minutes.

6. Let the pressure release naturally for 10 minutes before quick releasing the remaining pressure and safely removing lid. Remove chops to rest under tin foil for 5 minutes before serving. Serve with a spoonful of cooking liquid poured over top to moisten.

Bob's Tips

Lighter side dishes go best with the strong flavors of the olive and wine. Steamed vegetables and parsley or mashed potatoes would make a wonderful meal.

VEAL/LAMB

Prep Time	Cook Time		Serves	Temperature
15 MINS	6 MINS		FOUR	HIGH

VEAL FRANCAISE

VEAL AND LAMB

T HIS RECIPE FOR VEAL IN A LEMON BUTTER sauce is French cooking at its most basic. If I've learned anything, it's that with a little butter you too can be a French chef. If you're a margarine person however, I don't have anything clever to say about that!

1. DIP veal scallopini in seasoned flour until they are well coated.

2. POUR the olive oil and butter into the pressure cooker and heat on high or "brown" with the lid off, until sizzling.

3. ADD garlic and veal to pressure cooker, browning each piece on both sides before adding in remaining ingredients, except for the corn starch.

4. SECURELY lock on the pressure cooker's lid, set the cooker to high and cook for 6 minutes.

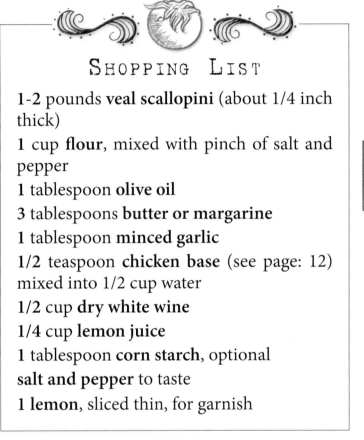

SHOPPING LIST

1-2 pounds **veal scallopini** (about 1/4 inch thick)

1 cup **flour**, mixed with pinch of salt and pepper

1 tablespoon **olive oil**

3 tablespoons **butter or margarine**

1 tablespoon **minced garlic**

1/2 teaspoon **chicken base** (see page: 12) mixed into 1/2 cup water

1/2 cup **dry white wine**

1/4 cup **lemon juice**

1 tablespoon **corn starch**, optional

salt and pepper to taste

1 **lemon**, sliced thin, for garnish

5. LET the pressure release naturally for 5 minutes before quick releasing the remaining pressure and safely removing lid.

6. SALT and pepper to taste and serve with pasta or potatoes, drizzled with the cooking liquid and garnished with lemon. To thicken the cooking liquid into a heartier sauce: remove veal from cooker, setting aside under tin foil to keep warm. Combine 1 tablespoon corn starch with 2 tablespoons water in a small dish and then stir into the cooker on high or brown, with lid off, simmering until thick. Return veal to cooker to coat well before serving.

Bob's Tips

Many grocery stores sell thinly sliced veal scallopini, but if yours does not, don't let that dissuade you. Veal cutlets can be pounded down to 1/4 inch thick for this recipe by sandwiching the cutlets between two sheets of plastic wrap on a sturdy cutting board and hammering with a mallet.

COOKING TIMES
SEAFOOD

WHEN COOKING SEAFOOD, quick releasing the pressure is a must. Thicker filets of fish and larger shrimp or scallops are recommended as seafood is very delicate. Cooking on a metal pressure cooker rack is also recommended. Add 1 minute to the cooking times if using frozen.

SEAFOOD	LIQUID	COOK MINUTES	TEMP
CLAMS	1/2 cup	5	high
COD	1/2 cup	4	high
CRAB LEGS, SMALL	1/2 cup	2	high
LOBSTER TAIL, 1/2 POUND	1/2 cup	5	high
MUSSELS	1/2 cup	3	high
SALMON	1/2 cup	6	high
SCALLOPS, BAY	1/2 cup	1	high
SCALLOPS, SEA	1/2 cup	2	high
SHRIMP	1/2 cup	2	high

SEAFOOD

Prep Time	Cook Time	Serves	Temperature
15 MINS	10 MINS	EIGHT	HIGH

PAELLA

SEAFOOD

MUCH LIKE A STEW OR A GUMBO, THIS Spanish rice dish can come in any number of variations. This particular variation would be known as a mixed paella, as it includes chicken, sausage and seafood. Paella's characteristic yellow coloring comes from saffron, the world's most expensive spice by weight… of course, for this recipe you only need 5 thread thin strands!

1. MIX saffron strands into 2 tablespoons warm water in a small dish and let sit for at least 20 minutes.

2. ADD the olive oil, garlic and sausage to pressure cooker and cook on high or "brown" with lid off, breaking up sausage into small pieces with a spatula.

3. ADD the chicken, onion and rice to cooker and stir around until rice is fully coated with oil and chicken begins to turn white.

4. COVER with saffron strands in water and remaining ingredients, except for shrimp, scallops, bell pepper and parsley. Securely lock on the pressure cooker's lid, set the cooker to high and cook for 8 minutes.

SHOPPING LIST

5 strands **saffron**
3 tablespoons **olive oil**
1 tablespoon **minced garlic**
1/2 pound **chorizo sausage**
1 pound **boneless, skinless chicken thighs**, each thigh cut into 3 strips
1 **onion**, diced
2 cups **short grain white rice**, uncooked
1 can **stewed tomatoes**, drained well
4 teaspoons **chicken base** (see page: 12) mixed into 4 cups water
1/2 cup **dry white wine**
zest of **1 lemon**
1 **bay leaf**
1/2 pound **shrimp**, shelled and deveined
1/2 pound **scallops**
1 **red bell pepper**, diced
parsley, for garnish
salt and pepper to taste

5. PERFORM a quick release to release the cooker's pressure before safely removing the lid. Stir in shrimp, scallops and bell pepper, then re-secure the lid, set the cooker to high and cook for 2 additional minutes.

6. PERFORM a quick release to release the cooker's pressure before safely removing the lid. Salt and pepper to taste and garnish with parsley before serving.

Many variations of Paella include mussels, but with this many other ingredients involved, mussels may not fit in your pressure cooker. You can always cook them separately and add them to the dish at the end. Scrub and de-beard them well, then simmer them in a large, covered pan with 1 1/2 cups white wine for 5 minutes until they open.

PREP TIME	COOK TIME		SERVES	TEMPERATURE
5 MINS	6 MINS		FOUR	HIGH

HONEY PECAN SALMON STEAKS

SEAFOOD

PECANS ARE THE ONLY THING I LOVE more on salmon than honey, but with this recipe I get them both! Thicker than a glaze, the topping on these thick cut salmon steaks is unbelievably easy to put together and unendingly brag-worthy.

1. ADD water to pressure cooker and lay salmon steaks over top.

2. COMBINE remaining ingredients in a small bowl and then spoon the mixture equally across the tops of all 4 salmon steaks.

3. SECURELY lock on the pressure cooker's lid, set the cooker to high and cook for 6 minutes.

4. PERFORM a quick release to release the cooker's pressure and safely remove lid. Use a spatula to serve immediately.

SHOPPING LIST

1/2 cup **water**

4 thick cut **salmon steaks**, about 1 inch thick

2 tablespoons **butter**, melted

1 tablespoon **honey**

3 tablespoons **whole grain mustard**

1/4 cup **pecans**, chopped fine

2 teaspoons **light brown sugar**

2 teaspoons **parsley flakes**

salt and pepper to taste

 I like to serve this with sautéed carrots and rice pilaf or jasmine rice, but it would also go well with fingerling or new potatoes.

Prep Time	Cook Time		Serves	Temperature
5 MINS	2 MINS		FOUR	HIGH

SHRIMP SCAMPI

SEAFOOD

THIS GRATIFYING OVERLOAD OF GARLIC, butter and wine is one of those recipes that's popularity is so broad that it needs no introduction. Okay, enjoy.

1. ADD all ingredients to pressure cooker and securely lock on the lid. Set the cooker to high and cook for 2 minutes.

2. PERFORM a quick release to release the cooker's pressure and safely remove lid. Salt and pepper to taste.

SHOPPING LIST

1 pound **shrimp**, peeled and deveined

4 tablespoons **butter or margarine**

2 tablespoons **minced garlic**

3/4 cup **dry white wine**

1 tablespoon **lemon juice**

1/4 teaspoon **paprika**

2 teaspoons **parsley**, chopped

salt and pepper to taste

shredded Parmesan cheese, for garnish

3. SERVE over linguine or your favorite pasta, topped with shredded or shaved Parmesan cheese.

Bob's Tips It should go without saying that a recipe is only the sum of its ingredients. A good quality white wine can make all the difference in a recipe like this. Somebody once said to me, "If you wouldn't drink it, don't cook with it!" and I've adhered to that ever since. The good thing is that there are some very good wines in the $7-$10 range these days.

Prep Time	Cook Time		Serves	Temperature
10 MINS	2 MINS		FOUR	HIGH

MEDITERRANEAN SCALLOPS

SEAFOOD

THIS SCALLOP DISH IS A LIGHT AND delicious taste of Italy and Greece effortlessly delivered to your table in only 12 minutes. With Roma tomatoes and feta cheese, I'll let you figure out which country each influence is from!

1. RINSE the scallops well.

2. ADD tomatoes to the pressure cooker, and then layer the scallops over top of them.

3. COVER with remaining ingredients, except the feta cheese and securely lock on the pressure cooker's lid. Set the cooker to high and cook for 2 minutes.

SHOPPING LIST

1 pound **scallops**

6 **Roma or plum tomatoes**, chopped large

2 tablespoons **olive oil**

2 tablespoons **butter or margarine**

2 teaspoons **minced garlic**

1/2 **red onion**, diced

1/2 cup **dry white wine**

1 tablespoon **lemon juice**

1 teaspoon **oregano**

1/2 cup **feta cheese**

salt and pepper to taste

4. PERFORM a quick release to release the cooker's pressure and safely removing lid. Salt and pepper to taste. Serve over your favorite pasta, topped with feta cheese.

 This recipe goes great with delicate pasta like angel hair or even orzo. If you'd prefer, shrimp can easily be substituted in place of the scallops—or use 3/4 pound of each for a Mediterranean Seafood Pasta because two is always better than one!

Prep Time	Cook Time	Serves	Temperature
10 MINS	3 MINS	FOUR	HIGH

Mussels Fra Diavolo

Seafood

This Italian dish of mussels, stewed tomatoes and a little bit of heat is the perfect way to spice up your night. No need to wait for a special occasion to give these a try—though you may have to wait until you've built up the courage!

1. RINSE and de-beard mussels.

2. ADD all ingredients to pressure cooker, except for mussels and stir well.

3. ADD mussels on top of mixture in cooker and securely lock on the pressure cooker's lid. Set the cooker to high and cook for 3 minutes.

Shopping List

2 tablespoons **olive oil**

1 **onion**, chopped

2 teaspoons **minced garlic**

1 can **diced tomatoes** (14-16 ounces)

1/2 cup **dry white wine**

3 tablespoons **tomato paste**

1 teaspoon **Italian seasoning**

1/2 teaspoon **crushed red pepper**

1 tablespoon **fresh parsley**, chopped

2 pounds **mussels**

salt and pepper to taste

4. PERFORM a quick release to release the cooker's pressure and safely removing lid. Salt and pepper to taste. Serve over your favorite pasta, garnished with additional fresh parsley.

 For the true, and truly spicy, effect of a Fra Diavolo, throw in a fresh chili pepper or two.

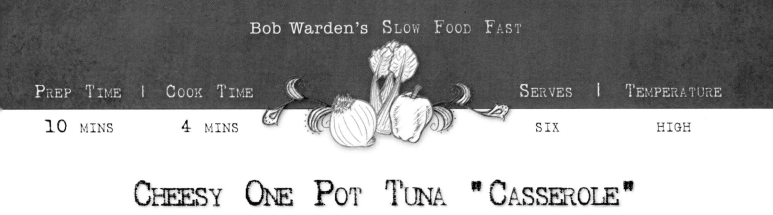

Prep Time	Cook Time		Serves	Temperature
10 MINS	4 MINS		SIX	HIGH

Cheesy One Pot Tuna "Casserole"

SEAFOOD

THIS DISH IS ANOTHER CLASSIC AMERICAN family style recipe that everyone in your house will love. It reminds me of a certain and helpful boxed dinner, but why make dinner from a box when you can make it fresh? Try this recipe for yourself and I am sure you'll be asking the same thing!

1. ADD egg noodles, chicken base mixed into water, tuna, bell pepper and butter to pressure cooker, securely lock on lid, set the cooker to high and cook for 4 minutes.

2. PERFORM a quick release to release the cooker's pressure. Safely remove lid and slowly stir in the Parmesan cheese, cheddar cheese, cream cheese and peas until cheeses are melted and creamy. Salt and pepper to taste and serve immediately, topped with cracker crumbs.

SHOPPING LIST

3 cups **egg noodles**, uncooked

3 teaspoons **chicken base** (see page: 12) mixed into 3 cups water

2 cans **white tuna**, drained well

1/2 **red bell pepper**, finely diced

2 tablespoons **butter or margarine**

1 tablespoon **grated Parmesan cheese**

1 cup **sharp cheddar cheese**

2 ounces **cream cheese** (1/4 regular sized brick)

1 cup **frozen peas**, thawed

1 cup **crackers**, crumbled (Ritz suggested)

salt and pepper to taste

SEAFOOD

Bob's Tips For something a little different try topping with crumbled sour cream and onion potato chips instead of crackers.

COOKING TIMES
BEANS AND LEGUMES

WHEN COOKING BEANS AND LEGUMES, do not fill your pressure cooker more than half full. All cooking times listed are for unsoaked beans. When cooking beans, add enough water to cover the beans and 2 tablespoons vegetable oil to prevent them from foaming. For firm beans, quick release the pressure. For soft, let the pressure release naturally.

BEANS	COOK MINUTES	TEMP
BLACK BEANS	20	high
BLACK-EYED PEAS	8	high
CANNELLINI	35	high
GARBANZO (CHICKPEAS)	35	high
GREAT NORTHERN	25	high
KIDNEY	22	high
LENTILS, GREEN	8	high
LENTILS, RED OR YELLOW	4	high
LIMA	12	high
NAVY	20	high
PEANUTS, RAW	60	high
PINTO	22	high
SCARLET RUNNER	16	high
SOY	28	high
SPLIT PEAS	6	high

Beans and Legumes

Prep Time	Cook Time		Serves	Temperature
10 MINS	9 MINS		EIGHT	HIGH

Black-Eyed Pea Salad with Bacon and Bell Pepper

Beans and Legumes

THIS CHILLED BLACK-EYED PEA SALAD is a refreshing alternative to an Italian pasta salad for your next party or family get together. The soft black-eyed peas are complemented perfectly by the crunchy raw bell pepper and smoky bacon. It's a simple, yet surprisingly new and unique picnic dish that is all prepped and ready to impress in minutes!

1. COMBINE the black-eyed peas, oil and spices in pressure cooker and add enough water to cover beans.

2. SECURELY lock on the pressure cooker's lid, set the cooker to high and cook for 9 minutes.

3. PERFORM a quick release, safely remove lid and test one of the peas for doneness. The peas should be firm enough to hold up being mixed into the salad without turning into a mash. If too firm for your taste, re-secure the lid and cook on high an additional 2 minutes.

SHOPPING LIST

BLACK-EYED PEAS

2 cups **black-eyed peas**

2 tablespoons **vegetable oil**, to prevent foaming

1/2 teaspoon **garlic powder**

1/2 teaspoon **onion powder**

1/2 teaspoon **Italian seasoning**

1/4 teaspoon **ground black pepper**

SALAD

1 **green bell pepper**, cored and finely diced

1 **yellow bell pepper**, cored and finely diced

1/2 cup **cooked bacon pieces** (can buy pre-cooked in salad dressing section)

1 cup **robust Italian salad dressing**

2 tablespoons **mayonnaise**

1/2 teaspoon **ground black pepper**

fresh parsley, for garnish

4. DRAIN the black-eyed peas into a colander and run cold water over them to cool them down. Combine with all salad ingredients, stirring well.

5. COVER and refrigerate for at least 2 hours before serving.

Though you can serve this as soon as it's chilled (or even as a warm salad), letting the salad marinate overnight really brings all of the flavors together in a truly great way. I always look for a good Italian dressing with plenty of spices and minced garlic at the bottom of the bottle for the best (and fastest) marinade.

Prep Time	Cook Time		Serves	Temperature
10 MINS	4 MINS		SIX	HIGH

One Pot Black Beans and Rice

Beans and Legumes

THIS TAKE ON A CUBAN CLASSIC IS ALL mixed up… literally. So simple, yet layered with flavors; serve this on its own as a vegetarian entrée or grill up some chicken skewers to lie over top. Throw a few sliced plantains on the grill for as close to an authentic Cuban meal as a farm boy like me knows anything about!

1. ADD olive oil, onion and bell pepper to the pressure cooker and heat on high or "brown" with the lid off for 5 minutes, until onions are almost completely translucent. Turn off or remove cooker from heat.

2. COVER with remaining ingredients, except for water and rice and stir well to combine. Pat the mixture down softly with a spoon to even it out.

3. SLOWLY pour water over top the bean mixture without stirring. Then pour rice over top everything.

Shopping List

2 tablespoons **olive oil**

1/2 **onion**

1/2 **green bell pepper**, diced

1 can **black beans** (14-16 ounces), with liquid

1 teaspoon **oregano**

1/4 teaspoon **sugar**

2 teaspoons **cider vinegar**

1/2 teaspoon **chicken base** (see page: 12) mixed into 1/2 cup water

1/4 teaspoon **cumin**

1/4 teaspoon **garlic powder**

2 1/2 cups **water**

1 1/2 cups **long grain white rice**, uncooked

salt and pepper to taste

4. SECURELY lock on the pressure cooker's lid, set the cooker to high and cook for 4 minutes.

5. LET the pressure release naturally for 5 minutes before quick releasing the remaining pressure and safely removing lid. Let cool for 5 minutes for rice to fluff up before serving.

If you'd prefer to keep things separate—serving the beans over the rice— follow the first two directions on the stove over medium high heat as you cook the water and rice in the pressure cooker on high for 4 minutes. Once the beans are bubbling, lower the stove to a simmer until the rice is ready.

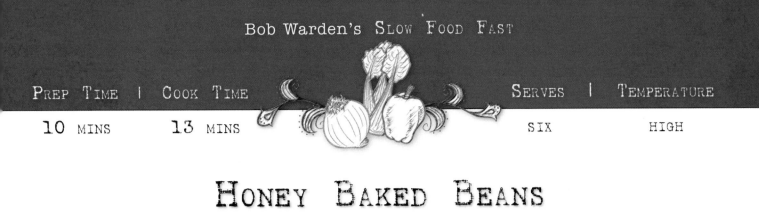

Prep Time	Cook Time			Serves	Temperature
10 MINS	13 MINS			SIX	HIGH

Honey Baked Beans

Beans and Legumes

THIS RECIPE FOR A BBQ AND PICNIC STAPLE uses honey instead of the molasses of more traditional baked beans. Just don't leave a batch lying around or a bee or two might bring the whole thing to their queen, bean by bean. Then they'd come for the burgers! This would probably not happen.

1. ADD the beans and vegetable oil to the pressure cooker and cover with water up to at least 1 1/2 inches above the beans. Securely lock on the pressure cooker's lid, set the cooker to high and cook for 10 minutes.

2. PERFORM a quick release to release the cooker's pressure and safely remove lid. Drain beans.

Shopping List

1 pound **dried white navy beans**, soaked for 6 hours

2 tablespoons **vegetable oil**

water to cover beans

2 tablespoons **ketchup**

1/4 cup **honey**

1/2 cup **light brown sugar**

1/2 teaspoon **garlic powder**

1/2 teaspoon **onion powder**

1 cup **water**

3. RETURN beans to pressure cooker, cover with ketchup, honey, brown sugar, garlic powder, onion powder and 1 cup water and stir well. Re-lock on pressure cooker's lid, set the cooker to high and cook for 3 minutes.

4. LET the pressure release naturally for 15 minutes before quick releasing any remaining pressure, safely removing lid and serving.

Replace the ketchup with a good BBQ sauce for beans with a bit more bang. Throw 1/4 cup of chopped raw bacon in with the beans in step 1 of the cooking process for something even better! Add sliced hot dogs in step 3 for that "beanie" childhood favorite with a rhyming name!

BEANS

Prep Time	Cook Time		Serves	Temperature
10 MINS	35 MINS		EIGHT	HIGH

Spinach and Artichoke Hummus

Beans and Legumes

FRESH HUMMUS IS A TRULY GREAT THING, but when the traditional is getting a little ho-hum, dip into this new take on two classics! Is it hummus? Is it spinach and artichoke dip? It's all the creaminess of both, but surprisingly different and in a very good way!

1. COMBINE the chickpeas, water, oil and salt in pressure cooker.

2. SECURELY lock on the pressure cooker's lid, set the cooker to high and cook for 35 minutes. Let the pressure release naturally.

3. SAFELY remove lid and drain the chickpeas into a colander. Cool the chickpeas to room temperature by running cold water over them.

4. SET ASIDE spinach, 1/4 jar of artichoke hearts and 1/2 of the jar's marinade and pour the remaining liquid and artichokes into a blender. Add chickpeas and all Hummus ingredients to blender.

SHOPPING LIST

CHICKPEAS

3 cups **dried chickpeas**

2 quarts **water**, or enough to cover chickpeas by two inches

2 tablespoons **vegetable oil**, to prevent foaming

1/2 teaspoon **salt**

HUMMUS

1 jar **marinated artichoke hearts** (12-14 ounces)

1 tablespoon **lemon juice**

1 tablespoon **minced garlic**

1/2 cup **Parmesan cheese**, grated or shredded

1 cup **fresh spinach leaves**

salt and pepper to taste

BEANS

5. BLEND on low, until you have a smooth, but still thick consistency. Add in more of the artichoke marinade until you've reached the desired texture. Stop the blender and salt to taste.

6. ADD in the remaining artichoke hearts and spinach and pulse the blender for only a few seconds until the spinach is broken up into pieces. Serve immediately, topped with more grated Parmesan cheese for garnish.

Though this isn't exactly your traditional hummus, feel free to serve it the traditional way with warm pita bread. I prefer grilling pita bread on an indoor grill, grill pan or Panini press. This is also great as a bruschetta (crusty Italian bread, thinly sliced and grilled) topping.

Prep Time	Cook Time		Serves	Temperature
5 MINS	7 MINS		SIX-EIGHT	HIGH

CURRIED LENTILS

BEANS AND LEGUMES

Lentils are an inexpensive (and protein packed) legume that don't have a very pronounced flavor. This recipe gets a major boost in the taste department with a good amount of curry. Serve them as a vegetarian entrée or the perfect side for any meal that could use a little pick me up.

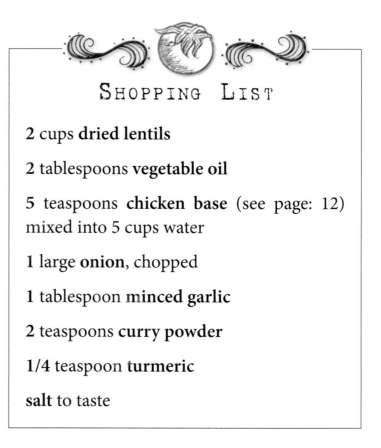

SHOPPING LIST

2 cups **dried lentils**

2 tablespoons **vegetable oil**

5 teaspoons **chicken base** (see page: 12) mixed into 5 cups water

1 large **onion**, chopped

1 tablespoon **minced garlic**

2 teaspoons **curry powder**

1/4 teaspoon **turmeric**

salt to taste

1. RINSE lentils in a colander, picking through them to make sure there are no stones or other objects.

2. ADD all ingredients to pressure cooker, stir and securely lock on lid. Set the cooker to high and cook for 7 minutes.

3. PERFORM a quick release to release the cooker's pressure and safely remove lid. Test lentils for doneness. If not to your liking, re-lock lid and cook on high for an additional 2 minutes. Salt to taste and serve with a slotted spoon.

Bob's Tips For a spicier curry, try adding a teaspoon of chili powder and ground ginger. For even spicier yet, throw in a pinch of cayenne pepper.

BEANS

Prep Time	Cook Time	Serves	Temperature
5 MINS	8 MINS	SIX	HIGH

Buttery Lima Beans with Sweet Bacon

Beans and Legumes

BELIEVE IT OR NOT, THIS LIMA BEAN recipe is a real crowd pleaser. With sweet brown sugar and savory bacon, lima beans don't even have to be your cup of tea to enjoy this dish! And you may just find that children will even eat a bean or two!

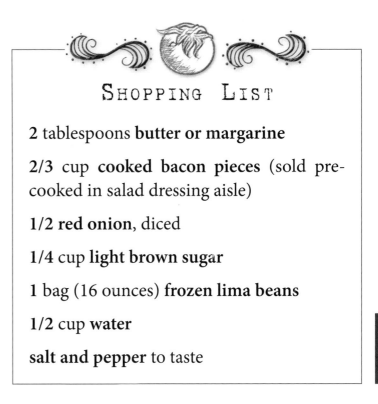

Shopping List

2 tablespoons **butter or margarine**

2/3 cup **cooked bacon pieces** (sold pre-cooked in salad dressing aisle)

1/2 **red onion**, diced

1/4 cup **light brown sugar**

1 bag (16 ounces) **frozen lima beans**

1/2 cup **water**

salt and pepper to taste

1. ADD the butter, bacon and red onion to the pressure cooker and heat on high or "brown" with the lid off for 3-4 minutes until onions begin to turn translucent.

2. ADD brown sugar to bacon and onions and stir well.

3. COVER with lima beans and water and securely lock on the pressure cooker's lid. Set the cooker to high and cook for 8 minutes.

4. PERFORM a quick release to release the cooker's pressure before safely removing lid. Salt and pepper to taste and serve.

Bob's Tips

I prefer to make this with the smaller "baby lima beans" but it can be made with any lima or butterbean, or pretty much any variety of frozen bean for that matter.

Prep Time	Cook Time		Serves	Temperature
5 MINS	55 MINS		EIGHT	HIGH

Southern Style Boiled Peanuts

Beans and Legumes

These boiled peanuts are a staple in the South where they are cooked up in copper pots or even giant drums on the side of the road. Cooked in much the same way as a bean, it's an entirely different take on peanuts that is soft, salty and incredibly irresistible. Traditionally, they are boiled in salt water for well over 4 hours to get to where the pressure cooker takes them in less than 1!

1. Combine the raw peanuts, salt and Cajun Style spices (if you would like) in pressure cooker and add enough water to cover peanuts.

Shopping List

1 1/2 pounds (24 ounces) **raw peanuts in shell** (usually sold in produce section)

1 tablespoon **vegetable oil**

4 tablespoons **salt**

<u>Cajun Style (optional)</u>

2 tablespoons **Old Bay seasoning**

1 teaspoon **garlic powder**

1 teaspoon **onion powder**

1 teaspoon **crushed red pepper flakes**

BEANS

2. Securely lock on the pressure cooker's lid, set the cooker to high and cook for 55 minutes.

3. Let the pressure release naturally for at least 10 minutes before quick releasing any remaining pressure to safely remove the lid and serve.

Bob's Tips

Though they are cooked in salt, boiled peanuts should be stored in their original cooking juice in the refrigerator and eaten within 3 or 4 days for best texture. I find that they have their best flavor after reheating in the microwave on day two.

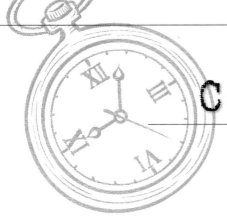

COOKING TIMES
VEGETABLES

WHEN COOKING VEGETABLES, quick releasing the pressure is an absolute must. Only let the pressure release naturally if you are planning on pureeing the result into a soup. Use a metal rack or steam basket for the crispest vegetables.

VEGETABLE	LIQUID	COOK MINUTES	TEMP
ACORN SQUASH, HALVED	1 cup	7	low
ARTICHOKE, WHOLE	1 cup	8	high
ASPARAGUS, THICK	1/2 cup	2	low
BEETS, 1/4 INCH SLICES	1/2 cup	5	high
BROCCOLI OR CAULIFLOWER	1/2 cup	2	low
BRUSSELS SPROUTS	1/2 cup	4	low
BUTTERNUT SQUASH, 1 INCH CHUNKS	1 cup	4	low
CABBAGE, QUARTERED	covered	3	low
CARROTS, BABY OR CHUNKS	1/2 cup	4	low
CORN ON THE COB	1 cup	2	low
EGGPLANT, 1/2 INCH CHUNKS	1/2 cup	3	low
GREEN BEANS	1/2 cup	2	low
PEAS	1/2 cup	1	low
POTATOES, WHOLE NEW	1 cup	5	high
RUTABAGA, 1 INCH CHUNKS	1 cup	5	high
TURNIP, 1 1/2 INCH SLICES	1/2 cup	2	low
ZUCCHINI	1/2 cup	1	low

VEGETABLES AND SIDE DISHES

Prep Time	Cook Time	Serves	Temperature
20 MINS	6 MINS	SIX	LOW

RATATOUILLE

VEGETABLES AND SIDE DISHES

THIS IS ANOTHER CLASSIC FRENCH RECIPE with a million variations to be made. Though it may seem like a lot of work at first, this is one of the easiest ratatouilles you'll find and at only 8 minutes under pressure, it's most certainly the fastest. Try slicing the tomatoes, zucchini, squash and eggplant into discs for something a little bit closer to the ratatouille you may have seen in a certain animated film!

1. ADD the olive oil and garlic to the pressure cooker and heat on high or "brown" with the lid off until sizzling.

2. ADD the onions and cook until they begin to sweat.

3. ADD the tomato paste and stir to thin it out. Add remaining ingredients, pouring the vegetable broth over top last. Securely lock on the pressure cooker's lid, set the cooker to low and cook for 6 minutes. Then let sit for 6 additional minutes as the pressure releases naturally.

SHOPPING LIST

4 tablespoons **olive oil**

2 tablespoons **minced garlic**

1 large **onion**, quartered, then thinly sliced

2 tablespoons **tomato paste**

1 **eggplant**, cut into 1 inch cubes

1 **green bell pepper**, cut into 1/2 inch square pieces

1 **red bell pepper**, cut into 1/2 inch square pieces

1 large **zucchini**, chopped large

1 large **yellow squash**, chopped large

2 **tomatoes**, chopped large

2 teaspoons **Italian seasoning**

1 teaspoon **salt**

1/2 teaspoon **ground black pepper**

1/2 cup **vegetable broth**

Parmesan cheese, for garnish

4. PERFORM a quick release to release the rest of the cooker's pressure before safely removing lid. Serve warm with freshly grated, shredded or shaved Parmesan cheese.

Bob's Tips

There is much debate over when ratatouille is at its best, either immediately after preparing while some flavors are still separate or refrigerated overnight when the flavors have melded together. I prefer it immediately because I didn't do all of that chopping to wait until tomorrow!

VEGGIES

Prep Time	Cook Time		Serves	Temperature
10 MINS	1 MIN		SIX	HIGH

Sweet Red Cabbage with Sour Apple

Vegetables and Side Dishes

This side dish is as simple and quick as it gets. The perfect accompaniment to a pork roast, chops or even some good barbecue; this recipe is like every great pork side—sauerkraut, coleslaw and applesauce—all in one.

1. ADD the butter to the pressure cooker and heat on high or "brown" with the lid off until sizzling. Add julienned apples and sauté for 2 minutes, stirring frequently.

2. COVER with remaining ingredients, except cabbage and stir well to combine.

Shopping List

1 tablespoon **butter or margarine**

2 **green (tart) apples**, peeled, quartered and julienned

4 tablespoons **light brown sugar**

1/2 cup **red wine vinegar**

1/4 cup **water**

1/4 teaspoon **ground black pepper**

1 head **red cabbage**, quartered and then sliced thin

3. ADD in cabbage and securely lock on the pressure cooker's lid. Set the cooker to high and cook for 1 minute.

4. PERFORM a quick release to release the cooker's pressure. Safely remove lid and let cool for five minutes before serving.

Bob's Tips To julienne peeled apples: cut four sides off of the apple as close to the core as you can get. You should be left with a cubed core that you can discard. Lay the four chunks of apple on their flat side and slice about 1/6 inch thick. Stack slices a few at a time and slice into 1/6 inch wide sticks.

VEGGIES

Prep Time	Cook Time	Serves	Temperature
10 MINS	5 MINS	SIX	LOW

Herb "Roasted" Summer Squash

Vegetables and Side Dishes

While summer squash such as the yellow (technically known as crookneck) squash and zucchini used in this recipe are extremely versatile ingredients, I always seem to fall back on this classic recipe. While this recipe would typically be roasted in the oven, the pressure cooker locks all of the flavors in well and without compromise.

1. Add all ingredients, except water to the pressure cooker and heat on high or "brown" with the lid off until onions cook down considerably and squash begin to brown.

2. Cover with the 1/2 cup water, securely lock on the pressure cooker's lid, set the cooker to low and cook for 5 minutes.

Shopping List

2 tablespoons **olive oil**

1 tablespoon **minced garlic**

1 **red onion**, quartered, then thinly sliced

2 **zucchini**, chopped large

2 **yellow squash**, chopped large

1/4 teaspoon **dried rosemary**

1/2 teaspoon **dried oregano**

2 teaspoons **parsley flakes**

1/2 teaspoon **salt**

1/4 teaspoon **ground black pepper**

1/2 cup **water**

3. Perform a quick release to release the cooker's pressure before safely removing lid and serving with your favorite entrée.

Thoroughly scrub squash under running water before chopping. Zucchini especially tends to carry a lot of grit on its rind that isn't always visible to the naked eye.

VEGGIES

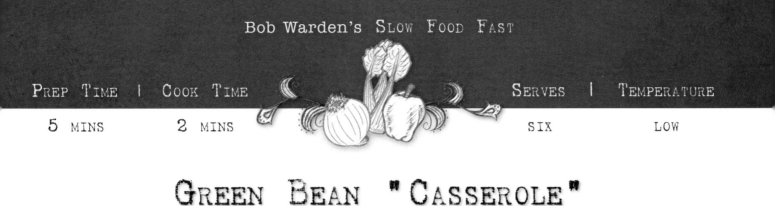

Prep Time	Cook Time		Serves	Temperature
5 Mins	2 Mins		Six	Low

Green Bean "Casserole"

Vegetables and Side Dishes

Eating a green bean casserole is probably the only time most people would dare get near a can of condensed cream of mushroom soup. I say, though it does make a good green bean casserole, this fresher, homemade version, is even better. With the help of the pressure cooker, the only thing condensed is the cooking time!

1. Add the butter, chopped mushrooms and garlic to the pressure cooker and heat on high or "brown" with the lid off until mushrooms have cooked down, about 3-4 minutes.

2. Cover with remaining ingredients except 2/3rds of the fried onions and sour cream. Securely lock on the pressure cooker's lid, set the cooker to low and cook for 2 minutes.

Shopping List

2 tablespoons **butter**

8 ounces **baby bella mushrooms**, finely chopped

1 tablespoon **minced garlic**

1 bag **frozen whole green beans** (16-22 ounces)

1/2 cup **vegetable broth**

1 **bay leaf**

1 can (3 ounces) **French fried onions**, split into 1/3 and 2/3 portions

16 ounces **reduced fat sour cream**

1 tablespoon **corn starch**, mixed into 1 tablespoon water

salt and pepper to taste

3. Perform a quick release to release the cooker's pressure before safely removing lid. Use a slotted spoon to transfer green beans to a casserole dish.

4. Set the cooker to high or "brown" with lid off and slowly stir in sour cream and corn starch mixed with water, simmering until thick. Salt and pepper to taste and then pour thickened sauce over green beans in casserole dish. Top with remaining fried onions and serve.

Bob's Tips

I like to buy "select" frozen green beans as they are almost indistinguishable from fresh without having to snap fresh beans for fifteen minutes. However, if you prefer, fresh are easily substituted. And if you really want to go homemade—try slicing thin, then sautéing 2 onions in 2 tablespoons butter until well caramelized for an onion topping that makes this an entirely different take on a classic.

VEGGIES

Prep Time	Cook Time		Serves	Temperature
10 MINS	2 MINS		FOUR	HIGH

Cauliflower with Cheese Sauce

Vegetables and Side Dishes

W HILE I MUST SAY THAT A GOOD CHEESE sauce is a sneaky way to get children to eat their vegetables, I should confess that cauliflower in a cheese sauce is one of my all time favorite sides, vegetable or not! This recipe is as quick and easy as I've ever made it—oh, and it's just as delicious as ever.

1. ADD all Cauliflower ingredients to pressure cooker, securely lock on lid, set the cooker to high and cook for 2 minutes.

2. PERFORM a quick release to release the cooker's pressure. Safely remove lid and slowly stir in the Cheese Sauce ingredients until melted and creamy. Salt and pepper to taste and serve immediately.

Shopping List

Cauliflower

1 head **cauliflower**, florets separated

1 1/2 teaspoons **chicken base** (see page: 12) mixed into 1 1/2 cups water

1 tablespoon **butter or margarine**

1 tablespoon **grated Parmesan cheese**

1/4 teaspoon **onion powder**

Cheese Sauce

1 cup **shredded sharp cheddar cheese**

2 ounces **cream cheese** (1/4 of a regular sized brick)

salt and pepper to taste

While the cauliflower holds up better to pressure cooking, broccoli florets can easily be substituted in this recipe, or even half cauliflower and half broccoli. Be careful when stirring in the cheese, as broccoli florets break up much easier and you don't want to end up with broccoli and cheese soup!

VEGGIES

Prep Time	Cook Time		Serves	Temperature
10 MINS	5 MINS		SIX	HIGH

Skillet Red Bliss Potatoes

Vegetables and Side Dishes

This is a perfect side dish to serve at a Sunday brunch for friends, maybe as an accompaniment to grilled salmon and asparagus. If you don't eat a meal like that outside on a picnic table under a shade tree, you don't know what you're missing.

1. Add the vegetable broth to the pressure cooker. For best results and firmer potatoes, position a steaming rack over broth.

2. Place potatoes into broth or onto steaming rack, securely lock on the pressure cooker's lid, set the cooker to high and cook for 5 minutes.

Shopping List

8 **red bliss potatoes**, cut in half

1 cup **vegetable broth**

1 tablespoon **olive oil**

2 tablespoons **butter**

1 teaspoon **minced garlic**

1 tablespoon **parsley flakes**

salt and pepper to taste

3. Perform a quick release to release the cooker's pressure, safely remove lid and drain the potatoes into a colander.

4. Add olive oil, butter, and garlic to pressure cooker and heat on high or "brown" with lid off until sizzling.

5. Return potatoes to cooker, with as many cut side down as possible, to brown. Brown the cut, flat side of the potatoes extremely well, until crispy. Add parsley, salt and pepper to taste before serving.

Add in a teaspoon of your favorite dried herb for "roasted" potatoes to match whichever dish you may be serving. Rosemary for beef. Marjoram for chicken. Oregano, thyme or dill... the possibilities are endless!

VEGGIES

Prep Time	Cook Time		Serves	Temperature
15 MINS	2 MINS		SIX	HIGH

REDSKIN POTATO SALAD WITH DILL

VEGETABLES AND SIDE DISHES

Whether you love traditional or German style potato salad, this secret recipe of mine will surely have you covered. It's a true original, with the fresh crunch of diced cucumber in place of the traditional celery. Cucumbers and dill, I wonder where I got that idea?

1. ADD the vegetable broth to the pressure cooker. For best results and firmer potatoes, position a steaming rack over broth.

2. PLACE cubed potatoes into broth or onto steaming rack, securely lock on the pressure cooker's lid, set the cooker to high and cook for 2 minutes.

3. PERFORM a quick release, safely remove lid and drain the potatoes into a colander. Run cold water over them to cool them down to room temperature.

SHOPPING LIST

Potatoes

6 red potatoes (about 2 pounds), cut into 1/2 inch cubes

1 cup **vegetable broth**

Salad

1/2 **onion**, diced small

1 small **cucumber**, chopped small

1/2 cup **mayonnaise**

1/2 cup **sour cream**

2 tablespoons **white vinegar**

2 tablespoons **fresh dill**, chopped

1/2 teaspoon **garlic powder**

salt and pepper to taste

4. FOLD potatoes into all salad ingredients slowly, careful not to mash them.

5. SALT and pepper to taste, then cover and refrigerate for at least 2 hours before serving.

Though you can serve this as soon as it's chilled (or even as a warm salad), the longer you let the salad marinate, the better. Try adding a tablespoon of sweet relish for a sweet contrast to this savory salad. When sweet and salty go head to head, you can do no wrong!

VEGGIES

Prep Time	Cook Time		Serves	Temperature
5 MINS	2 MINS		SIX	HIGH

MAPLE BUTTER GLAZED CARROTS

VEGETABLES AND SIDE DISHES

ANYTIME YOU CAN MAKE A VEGETABLE taste like dessert and get away with it, you've got a winner. Adults will appreciate the subtlety of the maple and cinnamon; children will simply ask for more.

1. ADD all ingredients except maple syrup and corn starch to pressure cooker and securely lock on lid. Set the cooker to high and cook for 2 minutes.

2. PERFORM a quick release to release the cooker's pressure and safely remove lid.

3. SET the cooker to high or "brown" with lid off and slowly stir in maple syrup and corn starch mixed with water, stirring until liquid is thick enough to thoroughly coat carrots. Serve immediately.

SHOPPING LIST

2 tablespoons **butter or margarine**

3 cups **baby carrots**

1/2 cup **water**

1 tablespoon **light brown sugar**

1/2 teaspoon **salt**

1/4 teaspoon **cinnamon**

1/4 cup **maple syrup**

2 teaspoons **corn starch**, mixed into 1 tablespoon water

Though baby carrots are easiest with no need to peel and chop, you can of course use 3 cups of regular sliced carrots. Be sure to slice the carrots thick, at least 1/4 of an inch to hold up best under pressure.

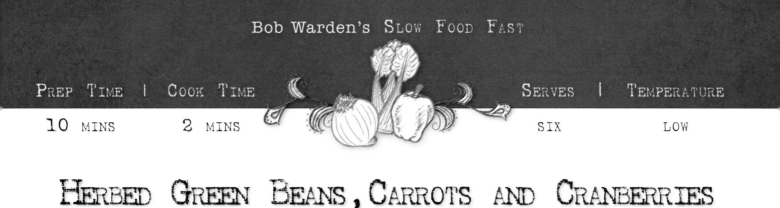

Prep Time	Cook Time	Serves	Temperature
10 MINS	2 MINS	SIX	LOW

Herbed Green Beans, Carrots and Cranberries

Vegetables and Side Dishes

There is no need to let your sides sit under tin foil to keep warm when you can cook up this holiday hit in only 2 minutes time! Prepare the ingredients in the pressure cooker's removable pot (or cooker itself for stovetop cookers) in advance and refrigerate covered until the rest of the meal is nearly ready and you're set to cook them up fresh, fast and just in time!

1. ADD all ingredients, except dried cranberries to the pressure cooker and stir.

2. SECURELY lock on the lid, set the cooker to low and cook for 2 minutes.

Shopping List

3 tablespoons **butter**

1 tablespoon **minced garlic**

1 bag **frozen whole green beans** (16-22 ounces)

1 1/2 cups **carrots**, peeled and julienned

1/2 cup **vegetable broth**

1 teaspoon **Italian seasoning**

1 tablespoon **parsley flakes**

1/2 teaspoon **onion powder**

1/2 cup **dried cranberries** (such as Craisins)

salt and pepper to taste

VEGGIES

3. PERFORM a quick release to release the cooker's pressure before safely removing lid. Stir in dried cranberries, then salt and pepper to taste. Let mixture cool for 2-3 minutes as the cranberries soften. Serve with a slotted spoon.

To julienne carrots: peel and cut in half. Lay halves down on their flat side and slice lengthwise into slices about 1/6 inch thick. Stack slices a few at a time and slice into 1/6 inch wide sticks.

Prep Time	Cook Time		Serves	Temperature
5 MINS	3 MINS		FOUR	HIGH

"Kettle" Sweet Corn on the Cob

Vegetables and Side Dishes

This recipe for corn on the cob reminds me of the salty/sweet carnival style kettle corn that seems to be everywhere these days! We've all had that great ear of corn that was as sweet as candy, but we can't always get that from our local grocery store so the added sugar here, infused at high pressure, guarantees greatness!

Shopping List

1 cup **water**

1/4 cup **sugar**

4 ears **fresh corn**, husked

2 tablespoons **butter or margarine**

1 teaspoon **salt**

1. ADD the water and sugar to the pressure cooker, and then position a rack over water.

2. PLACE ears of corn on rack as separated from each other as you have room (It's okay if they have to overlap.)

3. CUT butter into 4 equal pads and place one on each ear of corn.

4. GENEROUSLY sprinkle each ear of corn with salt.

5. SECURELY lock on the pressure cooker's lid, set the cooker to high and cook for 3 minutes.

6. PERFORM a quick release to release the cooker's pressure. Safely remove lid and serve.

Though you add butter before cooking, when corn on the cob is on the table, it's always a good idea to have more butter and salt nearby!

VEGGIES

Prep Time	Cook Time	Serves	Temperature
10 MINS	2 MINS	SIX	HIGH

LOADED SCALLOPED POTATOES

VEGETABLES AND SIDE DISHES

THIS IS ONE OF THOSE FLAVORS YOU GET a craving for and you can't rest until you get it. Fortunately, this recipe makes it simple to satisfy your basic human need for cheese and bacon without having to find a restaurant that still has potato skins on the menu.

1. ADD the sliced potatoes, chicken base mixed with water and bacon pieces to the pressure cooker. Securely lock on the lid, set the cooker to high and cook for 2 minutes.

2. PERFORM a quick release to release the cooker's pressure. Safely remove lid and slowly stir in the cheddar and cream cheese until melted and creamy. Salt and pepper to taste and serve immediately.

SHOPPING LIST

6 redskin potatoes, sliced into 1/6 inch slices

1 teaspoon **chicken base** (see page: 12) mixed into 1 cup water

1/2 cup **cooked bacon pieces** (can be purchased in salad dressing aisle)

1/2 cup **shredded sharp cheddar cheese**

2 ounces **cream cheese** (1/4 regular sized brick)

salt and pepper to taste

Try substituting diced ham in place of the bacon pieces and adding chopped broccoli florets during the first step of cooking to make a 2 minute potato casserole dinner!

VEGGIES

Prep Time	Cook Time		Serves	Temperature
10 MINS	4 MINS		SIX	HIGH

Candied Sweet Potatoes with Pecans

Vegetables and Side Dishes

This side dish is like a little bit of dessert smack dab in the middle of dinner. It's like maple syrup and sweet potatoes were meant to be together, then the pecan came along and created a dish fit for any holiday or just any day at all.

1. Toss the cubed sweet potatoes in corn starch until they are evenly coated (shaking in a plastic storage bag works best).

2. PLACE coated potatoes in pressure cooker, cover with remaining ingredients, except for pecans and stir.

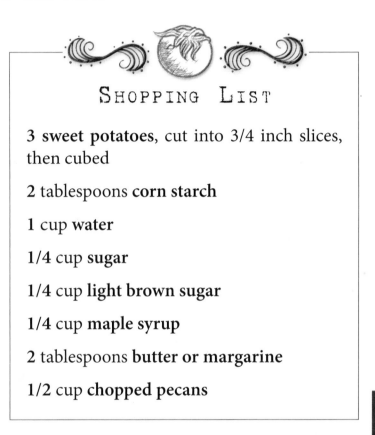

Shopping List

3 **sweet potatoes**, cut into 3/4 inch slices, then cubed

2 tablespoons **corn starch**

1 cup **water**

1/4 cup **sugar**

1/4 cup **light brown sugar**

1/4 cup **maple syrup**

2 tablespoons **butter or margarine**

1/2 cup **chopped pecans**

3. SECURELY lock on the pressure cooker's lid, set the cooker to high and cook for 4 minutes.

4. PERFORM a quick release to release the cooker's pressure. Safely remove lid and stir in chopped pecans before serving.

. Mash. Add crushed pineapple, vanilla extract & cinnamon.

Bob's Tips

Transfer the potatoes into a casserole dish, top with a layer of marshmallows and place under the broiler until the marshmallows begin to brown and you've got the fastest sweet potato casserole you've ever made!

Prep Time	Cook Time		Serves	Temperature
5 MINS	2 MINS		FOUR	HIGH

Hominy Breakfast Hash with Ham

Vegetables and Side Dishes

Hominy is an all too often overlooked side dish and when it comes to pressure cookers, breakfast is an all too often overlooked meal. The dried, then soaked corn kernels may not seem like it at first, but do make the perfect accompaniment to an egg breakfast as they're most similar in taste and texture to Southern grits. This hominy hash with ham is a simple and quick way to kick off your day!

1. BREAK apart any clumps of hominy and add to pressure cooker.

2. COVER with remaining ingredients, except for chives, Colby-jack cheese and eggs and securely lock on the pressure cooker's lid. Set the cooker to high and cook for 2 minutes.

Shopping List

1 can **hominy** (14-16 ounces), drained and rinsed

2 tablespoons **butter or margarine**

1/2 teaspoon **chicken base** (see page: 12) mixed into 1/2 cup water

1/2 cup **cubed or diced ham** (many stores sell already cubed or diced)

1/4 teaspoon **garlic powder**

1/4 teaspoon **onion powder**

1/4 teaspoon **ground black pepper**

2 tablespoons **chives**, chopped

1/2 cup **shredded Colby-jack cheese**, optional

4 **eggs**, optional

3. LET the pressure release naturally for 5 minutes before quick releasing the remaining pressure and safely removing lid. Stir in chopped chives and plate each serving topped with shredded Colby-jack cheese and an egg cooked sunny side up or over easy.

Bob's Tips

Hominy comes in both white and yellow varieties. Both are extremely similar in taste, but I prefer to use white in this recipe for no other reason than it better contrasting the yellow of the cheese and egg yolk.

VEGGIES

COOKING TIMES
RICE

WHEN COOKING RICE, do not fill the pressure cooker with any more than 3 cups of dry rice. The following chart lists the ratio for 1 cup of rice to water, but you may double or triple it. Add 2 tablespoons of vegetable oil to prevent foaming. Rice should be rinsed well before cooking, unless you are making short grain risottos or sticky rice. Let the pressure release naturally for fluffy rice. Quick release the pressure for firmer rice. 1 cup dry rice makes around 3 cups cooked.

WHITE RICE	AMOUNT	LIQUID	COOK MINUTES	TEMP
SHORT GRAIN	1 cup	2 1/2 cups	7	high
MEDIUM GRAIN	1 cup	2 cups	6	high
LONG GRAIN	1 cup	1 1/2 cups	4	high
BROWN RICE				
SHORT GRAIN	1 cup	2 cups	14	high
MEDIUM GRAIN	1 cup	2 cups	14	high
LONG GRAIN	1 cup	2 cups	10	high
WILD RICE	1 cup	3 1/2 cups	20	high

RICE AND RISOTTO

RICE

Prep Time	Cook Time			Serves	Temperature
10 MINS	7 MINS			SIX	HIGH

ASPARAGUS RISOTTO

RICE AND RISOTTO

BEFORE I STARTED PRESSURE COOKING, risottos were always a mystery that I was sure only world class chefs could crack. Now, I'm not saying that your pressure cooker gave you a culinary degree, but this rich and creamy Asparagus Risotto sure tastes like it has!

1. TRIM about 1 1/2 to 2 inches off of the bottom, tough end of the asparagus and discard.

2. TRIM off the asparagus tips, about 1 1/2 inches from the top and place into a microwave safe dish. You should be left with the middle section of the asparagus stalks.

3. CHOP the stalks into 1/2 inch lengths.

4. ADD the oil, butter and minced garlic to the pressure cooker and heat on high or "brown" with the lid off, stirring constantly until sizzling.

5. ADD rice and asparagus stalk pieces from step 3 and stir constantly for 1 minute.

6. ADD remaining ingredients, except for Parmesan cheese and asparagus tips. Securely lock on the pressure cooker's lid, set the cooker to high and cook for 7 minutes.

7. WHILE the risotto is cooking, add water to the microwave safe dish of asparagus tips, enough that they are completely submerged. Microwave for 2-3 minutes until tips are tender but not mushy. Drain water.

8. WHEN risotto is done, perform a quick release to release the cooker's pressure. Safely remove lid, stir in Parmesan cheese and asparagus tips. Salt and pepper to taste and serve immediately.

SHOPPING LIST

1 pound **fresh asparagus**

1 tablespoon **olive oil**

2 tablespoons **butter or margarine**

1 tablespoon **minced garlic**

2 cups **Arborio or Calrose rice**

4 cups **vegetable broth**

1 cup **dry white wine**

1 teaspoon **lemon juice**

1/4 cup **Parmesan cheese**, grated or shredded

salt and pepper to taste

RICE

Bob's Tips

Most asparagus is shrink wrapped in a foam tray and the easiest way to cut the crunchy and inedible bottoms off is to place the wrapped foam tray on a cutting board and carefully chop through the entire package and all stalks in one swipe.

Prep Time	Cook Time		Serves	Temperature
15 MINS	5 MINS		SIX	HIGH

JAMBALAYA

RICE AND RISOTTO

Put on some zydeco tunes to play while you cook this Cajun favorite—I gare-on-tee that it will taste better. Your body may not be in New Orleans, but that doesn't mean that your heart and mind can't go!

1. Add the olive oil, garlic, sausage, onion, bell pepper and celery to pressure cooker and cook on high or "brown" with lid off until sausage begins to brown and vegetables begin to sweat.

2. Coat chicken thigh slices with the flour on all sides before adding them to the cooker.

3. Add the remaining ingredients, except for shrimp and green onion tops and stir. Securely lock on the pressure cooker's lid, set the cooker to high and cook for 5 minutes.

4. Perform a quick release to release the cooker's pressure and safely remove lid. Switch cooker to high or "brown" with lid off and stir in shrimp and green onion tops. Stir constantly until shrimp turn pink, about 3 minutes. Salt and pepper to taste and serve.

SHOPPING LIST

3 tablespoons **olive oil**

1 tablespoon **minced garlic**

1/2 pound **andouille or smoked sausage**, cut into 1/4 inch slices

1 cup **onion**, chopped large

1 **green bell pepper**, chopped large

2 stalks **celery**, chopped

1 pound **boneless, skinless chicken thighs**, each thigh cut into 3 strips

3 tablespoons **flour**

1 cup **long grain rice**, uncooked

2 teaspoons **chicken base** (see page: 12) mixed into 2 cups water

2 cans **stewed tomatoes** (14-16 ounces)

1 teaspoon **thyme**

1/2 teaspoon **paprika**

1/4 teaspoon **hot sauce** (Tobasco recommended)

1/4 teaspoon **cayenne pepper**

1 pound **shrimp**, peeled and deveined

1/4 cup **sliced green onion tops**

salt and pepper to taste

Bob's Tips

Jambalaya is probably the most open-ended and versatile dish of the south. Try replacing the sausage with ham and adding a can of black-eyed peas. And if you really like your spice, try adding fresh sliced jalapeño!

RICE

Prep Time	Cook Time		Serves	Temperature
10 mins	7 mins		six	high

Seared Cherry Tomato Risotto

Rice and Risotto

T HOUGH YOU CAN PRETTY MUCH PUT anything in or on top of a risotto and it will be delicious; there is definitely something special to a bitter/sweet pan seared cherry tomato. Serve it topped with a juicy grilled steak and you're in business. The markedly remarkable dinner business.

1. ADD the oil, butter, garlic and 1 cup of the cherry tomato halves (reserving the other 1/2 cup for garnish) to the pressure cooker and heat on high or "brown" with the lid off, stirring constantly until sizzling.

2. ADD rice and stir constantly for 1 minute to coat with oil.

Shopping List

1 tablespoon **olive oil**

2 tablespoons **butter or margarine**

1 tablespoon **minced garlic**

1 1/2 cups **cherry tomatoes**, halved

2 cups **Arborio or Calrose rice**

4 teaspoons **chicken base** (see page: 12) mixed into 4 cups water

1 tablespoon **dry red wine**

1 tablespoon **fresh basil**, chopped

1/4 cup **Parmesan cheese**, shredded

salt and pepper to taste

3. ADD remaining ingredients, except for Parmesan cheese, stir and securely lock on the pressure cooker's lid. Set the cooker to high and cook for 7 minutes.

4. PERFORM a quick release to release the cooker's pressure. Safely remove lid then salt and pepper to taste. Serve topped with reserved cherry tomato halves and shredded Parmesan cheese.

Stir in a cup of thawed frozen corn kernels right before serving, letting sit for 2 minutes to warm through for an extra sweet burst of flavor that both complements and contrasts the cherry tomatoes.

RICE

Prep Time	Cook Time		Serves	Temperature
5 MINS	25 MINS		SIX	HIGH

WILD RICE ALMONDINE

RICE AND RISOTTO

THIS WILD RICE DISH ALWAYS REMINDS me of the holidays! Though the dried cranberries are optional, I'd highly recommend them if you're cooking up poultry. The cranberries and almonds lend a sweet contrast to an otherwise savory side that will all but make the meal!

1. RINSE wild rice thoroughly before adding to pressure cooker.

2. ADD the butter, chicken base mixed with water, garlic powder, and onion powder to the pressure cooker and securely lock on the lid. Set the cooker to high and cook for 20 minutes.

3. PERFORM a quick release to release the cooker's pressure. Safely remove lid and stir in white rice and almond slivers. Lock on the pressure cooker's lid, set the cooker to high and cook an additional 5 minutes.

3. LET the pressure release naturally for 5 minutes before quick releasing the remaining pressure and safely removing lid. Immediately stir in parsley flakes and dried cranberries. Let the rice sit for 5 minutes to fluff up as cranberries soften slightly. Salt and pepper to taste and serve.

SHOPPING LIST

1 cup **wild rice**

3 tablespoons **butter or margarine**

3 1/2 teaspoons **chicken base** (see page: 12) mixed into 3 1/2 cups water

1/2 teaspoon **garlic powder**

1/2 teaspoon **onion powder**

1 cup **long grain white rice**

3/4 cup **blanched almond slivers** (sold in baking aisle)

1 tablespoon **parsley flakes**

1/2 cup **dried cranberries**, optional

salt and pepper to taste

RICE

Bob's Tips

Wild rice, at 25 minutes, has one of the longest cooking times of any grain in the pressure cooker. When you're cooking a holiday meal for family, you'll surely welcome the extra time to finish cooking other dishes! Also, as it takes longer to cook and overcook, it reheats well when prepared in advance.

Prep Time	Cook Time	Serves	Temperature
10 MINS	12 MINS	EIGHT	HIGH

Apple Brown Rice Stuffing

Rice and Risotto

This untraditional stuffing made from brown rice and apple makes a wonderful holiday side dish or even just the perfect accompaniment to a pork chop dinner. I just love pairing apples with poultry or pork, but don't always want a dab of applesauce running all over the plate!

1. PLACE the butter, apple and celery in the pressure cooker and heat on high or "brown" with the lid off, stirring constantly for 2-3 minutes until celery is sweating.

2. ADD rice and stir constantly for 1 minute to coat with butter.

3. ADD remaining ingredients and securely lock on the pressure cooker's lid. Set the cooker to high and cook for 12 minutes.

Shopping List

2 tablespoons **butter or margarine**

1 **apple**, peeled, cored and diced

2 stalks **celery**, diced

2 cups **long grain brown rice**, uncooked

2 teaspoons **chicken base** (see page: 12) mixed into 2 cups water

1 cup **apple juice**

1/2 teaspoon **poultry seasoning**

1/2 teaspoon **dried thyme**

1/2 teaspoon **onion powder**

1/8 teaspoon **cinnamon**

salt and pepper to taste

4. LET the pressure release naturally for 10 minutes before quick releasing the remaining pressure and safely removing lid. Salt and pepper to taste and serve.

To make this stuffing into a real holiday favorite, try stirring in 1/2 cup slivered almonds (sold in the baking aisle) and 1/4 cup raisins after pressure cooking and letting sit for 2-3 minutes to let the raisins soften slightly before serving.

RICE

Prep Time	Cook Time		Serves	Temperature
10 MINS	7 MINS		SIX	HIGH

PORTABELLA RISOTTO

RICE AND RISOTTO

GRAB A LOAF OF CRUSTY BREAD, A GLASS of wine and enjoy this earthy and satisfying risotto. Though it's hearty enough to eat as a full meal, a great risotto is at its best under lamb chops or veal.

1. PLACE the oil, butter, onion and chopped portabella mushrooms in the pressure cooker and heat on high or "brown" with the lid off, stirring constantly for 2 minutes, until mushrooms begin to cook down.

2. ADD rice and stir constantly for 1 minute to coat with oil.

3. ADD remaining ingredients, except for the Parmesan cheese and securely lock on the pressure cooker's lid. Set the cooker to high and cook for 7 minutes.

4. PERFORM a quick release to release the cooker's pressure. Safely remove lid and stir in Parmesan cheese. Salt and pepper to taste and serve immediately.

SHOPPING LIST

1 tablespoon **olive oil**

2 tablespoons **butter or margarine**

1/2 **red onion**, diced

2 large **portabella mushroom caps**, chopped

2 cups **Arborio or Calrose rice**

4 cups **vegetable broth**

1/2 cup **dry red wine**

2 teaspoons **dried thyme**

1/4 cup **Parmesan cheese**, grated

salt and pepper to taste

RICE

Bob's Tips

8 ounces of chopped baby bella mushrooms can easily be substituted for the large portabella mushroom caps without sacrificing any flavor. They seem to go on sale more often than their grown up counterparts.

PREP TIME	COOK TIME	SERVES	TEMPERATURE
5 MINS	7 MINS	SIX	HIGH

RISOTTO WITH GORGONZOLA AND WALNUTS

RICE AND RISOTTO

I CAN'T THINK OF ANY MORE PERFECT complement to a creamy risotto than a good quality, creamy Gorgonzola cheese. Try garnishing this with diced red apples to take this recipe to a whole different place! It's like a warm Waldorf salad and risotto all in one! The sweet apple perfectly contrasts the earthy walnuts and strong Gorgonzola cheese.

SHOPPING LIST

1 tablespoon **olive oil**

2 tablespoons **butter or margarine**

1 **onion**, diced

2 cups **Arborio or Calrose rice**

4 cups **vegetable broth**

1 cup **dry white wine**

1/4 cup **Parmesan cheese**, grated or shredded

6 ounces **Gorgonzola cheese crumbles** (may substitute any blue cheese)

1/2 cup **chopped walnuts**

salt and pepper to taste

1 **red apple**, diced, optional for garnish

1. ADD the oil, butter and diced onion to the pressure cooker and heat on high or "brown" with the lid off, stirring constantly until sizzling.

2. ADD rice and stir constantly for 1 minute.

3. ADD vegatable broth and white wine; securely lock on the pressure cooker's lid, set the cooker to high and cook for 7 minutes.

4. PERFORM a quick release to release the cooker's pressure. Safely remove lid, stir in Parmesan cheese, Gorgonzola cheese and chopped walnuts. Salt and pepper to taste, garnish with apple and serve immediately.

Toasted walnuts work best in this risotto. If you can only find raw walnuts in the store, preheat the oven to 350 degrees and place raw walnuts on a sheet pan, single layer. Bake for 10 minutes until you can smell the walnuts toasting.

RICE

Prep Time	Cook Time	Serves	Temperature
10 MINS	4 MINS	SIX	HIGH

Sesame Fried Rice

Rice and Risotto

THE DISTINCT FLAVOR OF SESAME OIL really sets this fried rice apart from the ordinary. No wok necessary, the rice is cooked and then fried right in the pressure cooker, scrambled egg and all. Pictured on page: 82.

1. ADD 2 tablespoons of the sesame oil, rice, water, soy sauce and chopped carrots to the pressure cooker and securely lock on lid. Set the cooker to high and cook for 4 minutes.

2. LET the pressure release naturally for 5 minutes before quick releasing the remaining pressure and safely removing lid.

Shopping List

4 tablespoons **sesame oil**, split into two 2 tablespoon portions

2 cups **long grain white rice**, uncooked

2 3/4 cups **water**

1/4 cup **low sodium soy sauce**

2 **carrots**, peeled and chopped

3/4 cup **frozen peas**

2 **eggs**, beaten

3. DRAIN excess liquid (for firmer rice) or let rice sit 5-10 minutes until all excess liquid has been absorbed.

4. STIR in remaining 2 tablespoons sesame oil and set cooker to high or "brown" with lid off.

5. ADD frozen peas and stir to combine. When the cooker has heated up enough to hear the rice sizzling, use a spoon to push the rice from the center outward, up against the walls of the cooker, until you've created a hole all the way to the bottom of the pot.

6. POUR the beaten eggs into the hole you created in the rice and let them cook as you would scrambled eggs, breaking them up and folding them into themselves until firm. Once firm and scrambled, stir to fully combine with rice and serve!

 Bob's Tips To substitute long grain brown rice in place of the white, up the cooking time from 4 minutes to 12 minutes.

Prep Time	Cook Time		Serves	Temperature
5 MINS	7 MINS		SIX	HIGH

Roasted Garlic and Lemon Risotto

Rice and Risotto

This savory risotto is a perfect complement to chicken, pork, or salmon. The roasted garlic is nutty without being overwhelming and the acidity of the lemon provides the perfect foil for the creamy richness of the risotto.

1. BLEND roasted garlic, lemon zest and white wine in a blender or food processor until a paste.

2. PLACE the oil, butter, and onion in the pressure cooker and heat on high or "brown" with the lid off, stirring constantly until onions sweat.

3. ADD rice and stir constantly for 1 minute to coat with oil.

Shopping List

10 cloves **garlic**, roasted

2 teaspoons **lemon zest**

1/2 cup **dry white wine**

1 tablespoon **olive oil**

2 tablespoons **butter or margarine**

1/2 **red onion**, diced

2 cups **Arborio or Calrose rice**

4 cups **vegetable broth**

1/4 cup **Parmesan cheese**, grated

2 tablespoons **parsley flakes**

salt and pepper to taste

4. ADD garlic paste mixture and vegetable broth, stir and securely lock on the pressure cooker's lid. Set the cooker to high and cook for 7 minutes.

5. PERFORM a quick release to release the cooker's pressure. Safely remove lid and stir in Parmesan cheese and parsley flakes. Salt and pepper to taste and serve immediately.

Nowadays, whole, peeled and separated garlic cloves are readily available in most grocery stores. They usually come in a plastic jar in the produce section. To roast them: preheat the oven to 400 degrees and line a baking sheet with foil. Lay garlic cloves out in a single layer and cover with another sheet of aluminum foil. Bake for 15-20 minutes until cloves turn a golden brown.

RICE

Cooking Times
Pasta

When cooking pasta, do not fill the pressure cooker with any more than 4 cups of dry pasta. Add enough water to cover pasta by at least 3 inches. Add 2 tablespoons of vegetable oil to prevent foaming. Drain after cooking. For couscous, add 1 1/2 cups of liquid for each cup of couscous and there is no need to drain. When cooking any pasta, quick releasing the pressure is a must.

Pasta	Cook Minutes	Temp
Farfalle	5	high
Couscous	2	high
Elbows	6	high
Fettuccine	6	high
Linguine	6	high
Orzo	4	high
Penne	7	high
Rotini	6	high
Tortellini, dried	5	high
Tortellini, fresh	3	high

PASTA

PREP TIME	COOK TIME	SERVES	TEMPERATURE
5 MINS	6 MINS	SIX	HIGH

MOST EXCELLENT MACARONI AND CHEESE

PASTA

Taking on the king of all comfort foods was no easy task for me and my pressure cooker. It took many trials and far too many errors to come out with a real winner of a dinner, but I think I've done it! All the creaminess you'd expect in under the time it used to take to boil pasta. It's proof positive that comfort food only needs to taste like you spent all day in the kitchen.

1. ADD all macaroni ingredients to pressure cooker, securely lock on lid, set the cooker to high and cook for 6 minutes.

SHOPPING LIST

Macaroni

2 1/2 cups **elbow macaroni**

2 teaspoons **chicken base** (see page: 12) mixed into 2 cups water

1 cup **water**

2 tablespoons **butter or margarine**

1 tablespoon **grated Parmesan cheese**

Cheese

2 cups **shredded sharp cheddar cheese**

2 ounces **cream cheese** (1/4 of a regular sized brick)

1 teaspoon **yellow mustard**

2. PERFORM a quick release to release the cooker's pressure. Safely remove lid and slowly stir in the cheese ingredients until melted and creamy. Serve immediately.

PASTA

Bob's Tips

I won't lie; sometimes I like to make this recipe with 2 cups of pasteurized cheese, such as Velveeta, instead of the cheddar and cream cheeses. For me, it's just as much a comfort food as macaroni and cheese itself! You can also run frozen broccoli florets under hot water for 2-3 until they've completely thawed and throw into the finished macaroni with cubed ham for a no bake casserole in minutes!

Prep Time	Cook Time		Serves	Temperature
10 MINS	4 MINS		FOUR-SIX	HIGH

ORZO PRIMAVERA

PASTA

THIS LIGHT AND REFRESHING PASTA DISH with a bevy of beautiful, brightly colored vegetables may just remind you of spring. It's no coincidence, as that's where Primavera gets its name! The small, almost rice sized orzo pasta is yet another breath of fresh air when you're tired of ordinary rice or pasta.

1. ADD the oil, butter, minced garlic and onions to the pressure cooker and heat on high or "brown" with the lid off, stirring constantly until sizzling.

2. COVER with remaining ingredients, except for Parmesan cheese. Securely lock on the pressure cooker's lid, set the cooker to high and cook for 4 minutes.

3. PERFORM a quick release to release the cooker's pressure, safely remove lid and stir in Parmesan cheese. Salt and pepper to taste and serve using a slotted spoon.

SHOPPING LIST

2 tablespoons **olive oil**

1 tablespoon **butter or margarine**

1 teaspoon **minced garlic**

1/2 **red onion**, diced

1 1/4 cup **orzo** (sold in pasta aisle)

3 teaspoons **chicken base** (see page: 12) mixed into 3 cups water

3 **carrots**, chopped small

1 cup **broccoli florets**, chopped into bite sized pieces

1/2 cup **red bell pepper**, chopped small

1 tablespoon **parsley flakes**

1/3 cup **Parmesan cheese**, grated or shredded

salt and pepper to taste

Bob's Tips — Though you can't find it in all stores, tricolored orzo pasta makes this lively dish even more vibrant. If orzo isn't readily available or just isn't your cup of tea, try 2 cups of bow-tie pasta in its place—extending the cooking time to 5 minutes under high pressure.

PASTA

Prep Time	Cook Time		Serves	Temperature
10 MINS	2 MINS		EIGHT	HIGH

Moroccan Couscous

Pasta

THIS RECIPE FOR COUSCOUS—TINY, almost granulated pasta—is a typical Moroccan preparation with chopped dates and cinnamon adding slight sweetness to this otherwise savory dish. For the best results, keep an eye out for regular uncooked couscous (usually sold in a clear plastic jar) not the instant variety that comes in a box.

1. PLACE the oil, onion, bell pepper and dates in the pressure cooker and heat on high or "brown" with the lid off, stirring constantly for 2-3 minutes until onions are sweating.

Shopping List

2 tablespoons **olive oil**

1/2 **onion**, diced

1/2 **red bell pepper**, diced

1/2 cup **dates**, chopped

2 cups **couscous**, uncooked

3 cups **vegetable broth**

1 tablespoon **lemon juice**

1 1/2 teaspoons **ground cinnamon**

salt and pepper to taste

2. ADD remaining ingredients and securely lock on the pressure cooker's lid. Set the cooker to high and cook for 2 minutes.

3. PERFORM a quick release to release the cooker's pressure and safely remove lid. Salt and pepper to taste and serve.

Bob's Tips

If you like spice, try adding 1/2 teaspoon cayenne pepper before cooking for a bit of a kick. I like to serve this garnished with chopped pecans or toasted almonds.

Prep Time	Cook Time		Serves	Temperature
5 MINS	7 MINS		SIX	HIGH

PENNE ALLA VODKA

PASTA

THIS PASTA HAS HAD A LITTLE TOO MUCH to drink and now it's blushing. An American Italian classic, Penne Alla Vodka combines a red and white sauce with a shot of its namesake alcohol for a distinctive flavor that's a knock-out punch guaranteed to leave you punch-drunk.

SHOPPING LIST

3 cups **penne pasta**, uncooked

1 1/2 cups **water**

1 jar store bought **marinara sauce** (24-26 ounces)

1 can **diced tomatoes** (14-16 ounces)

2 tablespoons **butter or margarine**

2 teaspoons **minced garlic**

1/4 cup **vodka**

1/2 cup **heavy cream**

1/4 cup **Parmesan cheese**

salt and pepper to taste

1. ADD all ingredients, except heavy cream and Parmesan cheese to pressure cooker and securely lock on the cooker's lid. Set the cooker to high and cook for 7 minutes.

2. PERFORM a quick release to release the cooker's pressure. Safely remove lid and slowly stir in the heavy cream and Parmesan cheese until melted and creamy. Salt and pepper to taste and serve immediately.

PASTA

Bob's Tips Skip the vodka and start off sautéing 1/2 a cup of diced bacon in the pressure cooker before step 1 in the recipe for a more family friendly dish that may just be better than the original!

Prep Time	Cook Time		Serves	Temperature
5 MINS	4 MINS		FOUR-SIX	HIGH

Cheese Tortellini Alfredo with Ham

Pasta

When you're feeding the whole family this is a grown up dish that the kids are guaranteed to love. And with so little prep time, it's something you can literally whip together in only ten minutes… another good thing when feeding a whole family!

1. Add all Tortellini ingredients to pressure cooker, securely lock on lid, set the cooker to high and cook for 4 minutes.

2. Perform a quick release to release the cooker's pressure. Safely remove lid and slowly stir in the Dairy ingredients until melted and creamy. Salt to taste and serve immediately.

Shopping List

Tortellini

1 large bag (13 ounces) **cheese tortellini**, dry (sold in pasta aisle)

1 1/2 cups **cubed or diced ham** (can buy already cubed in most stores)

2 1/2 cups **water**

3 tablespoons **butter or margarine**

1/2 teaspoon **garlic powder**

1/4 teaspoon **ground black pepper**

1/8 teaspoon **nutmeg**

Dairy

3/4 cup **grated Parmesan cheese**

3/4 cup **whole milk**

4 ounces **cream cheese** (1/2 regular sized brick)

salt to taste

PASTA

Bob's Tips If the sauce is too thin, add more cream cheese until you get the right consistency; too thick, just add more milk. Go full Italian by replacing the cubed ham with cooked, diced pancetta (Italian bacon) or try 2/3 of a cup of precooked bacon pieces, sold in the salad dressing aisle of your grocery store.

Prep Time	Cook Time		Serves	Temperature
10 MINS	6 MINS		FOUR	HIGH

Bacon Tomato Rotini with Peas

Pasta

THIS CREAMY ROTINI DISH IS FULL OF COLOR and flavor! Put together a salad while the pasta is cooking and you have a full meal in under 10 minutes for only a fraction of the price that you would spend at one of those big pasta restaurants.

1. ADD the rotini, chicken base in water, water and butter to the pressure cooker. Securely lock on lid, set the cooker to high and cook for 6 minutes.

2. PERFORM a quick release to release the cooker's pressure. Safely remove lid and slowly stir in the bacon pieces, Parmesan cheese and milk.

3. SET the cooker to high or "brown" with the lid off. Combine the corn starch with 2 tablespoons of water in a small dish and mix well. Slowly stir mixture into pressure cooker and simmer for 2 minutes after it begins to thicken.

4. STIR in tomatoes, peas and parsley. Salt and pepper to taste and serve immediately.

SHOPPING LIST

3 cups **rotini pasta**

2 teaspoons **chicken base (see page: 12)** mixed into 2 cups water

1 cup **water**

2 tablespoons **butter or margarine**

3/4 cup **cooked bacon pieces** (sold pre-cooked in salad dressing aisle)

1/2 cup **Parmesan cheese**

1 cup **milk**

2 tablespoons **corn starch**

2 **tomatoes**, chopped

1 cup **frozen peas**

2 teaspoons **parsley flakes**

salt and pepper to taste

Bob's Tips I make this dish with tri-color rotini, but penne pasta can be easily substituted. Mini penne pasta gives the dish a real restaurant quality presentation.

PASTA

SAUCES

Prep Time	Cook Time		Serves	Temperature
15 MINS	8 MINS		SIX	HIGH

BOLOGNESE SAUCE

SAUCES

THIS ITALIAN MEAT SAUCE IS SO VERSATILE, you may just want to make up two batches and freeze one for a rainy day! Of course, with only an 8 minute cook time you won't get much faster than just making it from scratch! I like this over petite penne pasta, but when it comes to meat sauce; it's hard to beat the classic comfort of spaghetti.

1. POUR the olive oil into the pressure cooker and heat on high or "brown" with the lid off, until sizzling.

2. ADD the onion and garlic and stir constantly for 1 minute.

3. ADD ground beef and Italian sausage to the pressure cooker and cook for 2 to 3 minutes, breaking the meat apart and browning well.

4. ADD remaining ingredients, securely lock on the pressure cooker's lid, set the cooker to high and cook for 8 minutes.

SHOPPING LIST

3 tablespoons **olive oil**

1 large **onion**, chopped large

1 tablespoon **minced garlic**

1 pound **ground beef**

1/4 **ground Italian sausage**, optional

1/4 cup **cooked bacon pieces** (can buy pre-cooked in salad dressing section)

1 can **diced tomatoes** (14-16 ounces)

1 can **tomato sauce** (14-16 ounces)

1/2 cup **dry white wine**

1 **bay leaf**

1 teaspoon **Italian seasoning**

1 teaspoon **parsley flakes**

1 teaspoon **sugar**

salt and pepper to taste

5. LET the pressure release naturally for 10 minutes before quick releasing the remaining pressure and safely removing lid. Salt and pepper to taste and serve over your favorite pasta.

For an amazing casserole, preheat the oven to 375 degrees and boil penne pasta on the stove while the sauce is cooking in the pressure cooker. Add cooked penne pasta to a casserole dish and cover with finished Bolognese sauce. Cover sauce with 2 cups of shredded mozzarella cheese and bake for 15 minutes until cheese is melted and bubbling. Let cool for 5 minutes before serving!

SAUCES

Prep Time	Cook Time			Serves	Temperature
10 MINS	0 MINS			SIX	NO COOK

Tzatziki Sauce

Sauces

Tzatziki Sauce is a Greek staple served with Gyros or my very own *Pork Souvlaki*, recipe page: 99. (Also pictured opposite that page.) This creamy yogurt sauce with cucumber and dill is a cool and refreshing contrast to any strongly herbed meat and the perfect "dip" for a warm piece of pita bread. Just don't tell the hummus!

SHOPPING LIST

1 medium **cucumber**

1 tablespoon **minced garlic**

1 tablespoon **lemon juice**

1 tablespoon **fresh dill**, chopped

2 cups **plain yogurt**

salt and pepper to taste

1. PEEL cucumber, and then slice in half lengthwise. Spoon out the softer, seed filled portion in the center and discard. Roughly chop the peeled and cleaned cucumber halves.

2. COMBINE all ingredients except yogurt in a food processor and pulse until well blended and cucumber is almost completely grated.

3. SKIM any liquid off the top of yogurt, and then combine with cucumber mixture until blended. Salt and pepper to taste, and then refrigerate for at least 2 hours before serving for best flavor.

Bob's Tips

The thicker consistency of Greek yogurt works best for this sauce, so keep an eye out for it in the dairy section of your grocery store. To make your own Greek yogurt, line a colander with 2 coffee filters (one right inside of the other) and place the colander over a bowl. Pour regular, plain yogurt into the coffee filters and refrigerate for 4 hours as the water drains out of the yogurt.

Prep Time	Cook Time	Serves	Temperature
10 MINS	5 MINS	SIX	HIGH

PUTTANESCA SAUCE

SAUCES

Puttanesca sauce, once an Italian way to utilize leftovers with a little of this and a little of that, its ingredients have somewhat standardized over time. A strong pasta sauce, most of its flavor comes from anchovy fillets that literally dissolve right into it as it cooks.

1. POUR the olive oil into the pressure cooker and heat on high or "brown" with the lid off, until sizzling.

2. ADD the garlic and anchovies and stir constantly until anchovies break apart entirely, almost dissolving.

3. ADD remaining ingredients, except for parsley flakes and securely lock on the pressure cooker's lid. Set the cooker to high and cook for 5 minutes.

4. LET the pressure release naturally for 5 minutes before quick releasing the remaining pressure and safely removing lid. Stir well to break apart tomatoes, add parsley flakes and serve over your favorite pasta.

SHOPPING LIST

3 tablespoons **olive oil**

1 tablespoon **minced garlic**

2 anchovy fillets

1 large can **whole tomatoes** (32 ounces)

1/4 cup **kalamata olives**, pitted and chopped

1 tablespoon **capers**

1/4 cup **dry red wine**

1/2 teaspoon **crushed red pepper**

1 teaspoon **dried basil**

1 tablespoon **parsley flakes**

Bob's Tips If anchovies aren't your thing, try replacing with 1/4 cup of diced pancetta (Italian bacon) or prosciutto (Italian ham). They carry their own, uniquely strong flavors, without anything fishy going on!

SAUCES

Prep Time	Cook Time	Serves	Temperature
5 MINS	4 MINS	SIXTEEN	LOW

Strawberry Sauce

Sauces

This simple strawberry sauce is a five minute, make ahead treat that is almost a prerequisite for your next *Vanilla Bean Cheesecake* (recipe page: 191). Whether you'd like to add a homemade touch to store bought ice cream or make the perfect strawberry shortcake, this sauce is as easy as it gets!

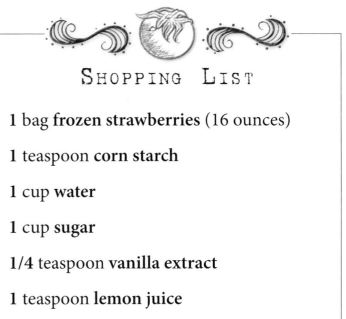

Shopping List

1 bag **frozen strawberries** (16 ounces)

1 teaspoon **corn starch**

1 cup **water**

1 cup **sugar**

1/4 teaspoon **vanilla extract**

1 teaspoon **lemon juice**

1. Cut open bag of frozen strawberries and add corn starch directly into bag. Hold bag closed and shake to lightly coat strawberries.

2. Add coated strawberries to pressure cooker, cover with remaining ingredients and stir.

3. Securely lock on the pressure cooker's lid, set the cooker to low and cook for 4 minutes.

4. Let the pressure release naturally for at least 10 minutes before slowly releasing the remaining pressure to safely remove lid. Keep your hand away from the steam as you release the remaining pressure, as it could spit the extremely hot sauce. Serve as a hot sundae topping or refrigerate for 2 hours to serve cold.

Bob's Tips

Though this recipe is easiest, most inexpensive and quite good with frozen strawberries, fresh are even better. Try substituting with two pints of fresh strawberries, tops removed. If the fresh strawberries are particularly good and sweet, you may want to cut the added sugar down from 1 cup to 3/4 of a cup.

SAUCES

Prep Time	Cook Time			Serves	Temperature
5 MINS	0 MINS			SIX-TEN	NO COOK

HORSERADISH CREAM

SAUCES

THIS LUXURIOUSLY CREAMY HORSERADISH sauce may bring a tear to your eye… literally. If you like it hot, than this one's for you. Serve with steaks, roast beef, corned beef or even as a fresh vegetable dip, if you dare!

SHOPPING LIST

1 cup **reduced fat sour cream**

2 tablespoons **horseradish**, jarred

1 tablespoon **Dijon mustard**

1/4 teaspoon **sugar**

salt and pepper to taste

1. COMBINE all ingredients in mixing bowl or food storage container and mix until well blended.

2. REFRIGERATE for at least 2 hours to unlock the most flavors before serving alongside your favorite dish.

Bob's Tips Serve with my recipe for Traditional Corned Beef and Cabbage, recipe page: 41. Or spread on a Kaiser roll piled high with thinly carved Perfect Pot Roast, recipe page 37.

SAUCES

Prep Time	Cook Time		Serves	Temperature
5 MINS	0 MINS		SIX-TEN	NO COOK

STICK TO YOUR RIBS BBQ SAUCE

Sauces

THIS NO COOK RECIPE FOR BBQ SAUCE is my tailor made secret to pressure cooking sweet and tangy barbecue dishes. It's made extra, extra thick to hold up well when combined with other liquids in pressure cooker recipes and when basting and re-basting your BBQ sauce just isn't an option.

1. COMBINE all ingredients in mixing bowl, large jar or food storage container and mix until well blended.

2. REFRIGERATE overnight to unlock the most flavors before using it to make your favorite pressure cooking barbecue dish.

SHOPPING LIST

2 cans **tomato paste** (6 ounces each)

1/3 cup **white vinegar**

1/4 cup **water**

3 tablespoons **light brown sugar**

1 tablespoon **molasses**

1 tablespoon **Dijon mustard**

1 teaspoon **liquid smoke**

1/2 teaspoon **paprika**

1 teaspoon **garlic powder**

1 teaspoon **onion powder**

1/2 teaspoon **celery salt**

1/4 teaspoon **ground black pepper**

small pinch **cinnamon**

Bob's Tips

This sauce is the perfect consistency for my BBQ Brisket, recipe page: 55. It can mix with the beer in the recipe without turning into water. Try topping a burger, or even meatloaf, with this sauce instead of ketchup to bring a little more flavor to the table!

SAUCES

Prep Time	Cook Time	Serves	Temperature
5 MINS	6 MINS	SIX	HIGH

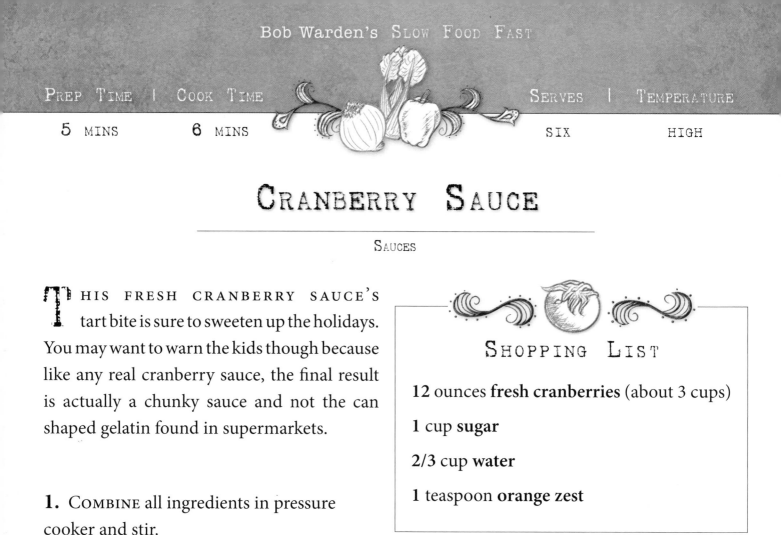

CRANBERRY SAUCE

SAUCES

THIS FRESH CRANBERRY SAUCE'S tart bite is sure to sweeten up the holidays. You may want to warn the kids though because like any real cranberry sauce, the final result is actually a chunky sauce and not the can shaped gelatin found in supermarkets.

SHOPPING LIST

12 ounces **fresh cranberries** (about 3 cups)

1 cup **sugar**

2/3 cup **water**

1 teaspoon **orange zest**

1. COMBINE all ingredients in pressure cooker and stir.

2. SECURELY lock on the pressure cooker's lid, set the cooker to high and cook for 6 minutes.

3. LET the pressure release naturally for 5 minutes before performing a quick release to release the remaining pressure and safely remove lid. Stir sauce, smashing cranberries until the sauce is at your desired consistency. Let sit an additional 5 minutes to firm slightly before serving warm.

Bob's Tips

Cranberries literally pop while they cook, so do not be alarmed if it sounds like you're making popcorn! People are pretty accustomed to a cold cranberry sauce these days which gives you plenty of time to prepare this before Turkey Day. The pectin in the cranberries will thicken the sauce even further after a few hours of refrigeration.

DESSERTS

Prep Time	Cook Time		Serves	Temperature
15 MINS	25 MINS		SIX	HIGH

Vanilla Bean Cheesecake

Desserts

With three forms of vanilla, it's safe to say that this cheesecake is anything but… vanilla. While keeping things simple enough to please classic cheesecake fans (which is a segment of the population that includes everyone) the fresh vanilla bean seeds speckled throughout is only slightly less impressive than the taste!

1. MIX cookie crumbs with butter and press into the bottom of a 7 inch springform pan to form the crust.

2. SLICE the vanilla bean lengthwise and scrape seeds into an electric mixer or food processor.

3. ADD cream cheese, sugar, eggs, yogurt, flour and vanilla extract to the electric mixer or food processor and mix on medium speed until mixture is well blended and fluffy.

SHOPPING LIST

1 cup **butter cookies**, crumbled
2 tablespoons **butter**
1 **vanilla bean**
16 ounces **cream cheese**, softened (2 regular sized bricks)
3/4 cup **sugar**
3 **eggs**
1/2 cup **vanilla yogurt**
1 tablespoon **flour**
1 teaspoon **vanilla extract**
2 1/2 cups **water**
whipped cream, to top

4. POUR the mixture over the crust in the springform pan. Tightly cover the pan with aluminum foil.

5. POUR water into the pressure cooker and place a metal rack at on the bottom. Place the springform pan on the rack.

6. SECURELY lock on the pressure cooker's lid and set the cooker to high for 25 minutes.

7. LET the pressure release naturally for 10 minutes before performing a quick release to release the remaining pressure. Safely remove lid, and let cool in the pressure cooker for 10 minutes before attempting to remove the pan. Do not attempt to remove the pan while still hot!

8. REFRIGERATE for 1 hour with aluminum foil off (blotting any water on the top of the cake with a paper towel to keep cake dry), then replace aluminum foil and refrigerate an additional minimum of 6 hours before serving topped with whipped cream.

It almost goes without saying that you should try this topped with Strawberry Sauce, recipe page: 185. Or serve it as is, topped with fresh vanilla beans for garnish.

DESSERTS

Prep Time	Cook Time		Serves	Temperature
15 MINS	15 MINS		FOUR	HIGH

Rum Raisin Bread Pudding

DESSERT

THIS HOLIDAY FAVORITE IS ANYTHING BUT a fruitcake. When it comes to this Rum Raisin Bread Pudding, I like to top it off with a scoop of vanilla ice cream and a drizzle of rum sauce, recipe in my tips below!

1. SPRAY a metal cake or pie pan (small enough to fit into the pressure cooker with room around the sides) with nonstick cooking spray and then add bread to pan.

2. ADD water bath water to pressure cooker and place cake or pie pan over top. For best results, place pan on top of a metal pressure cooker rack.

3. WHISK remaining ingredients in a mixing bowl until well blended and then pour into the cake or pie pan over the bread.

4. COVER cake or pie pan with aluminum foil, securely lock on the pressure cooker's lid and set the cooker to high for 15 minutes.

SHOPPING LIST

nonstick cooking spray
4 cups **French bread**, cut into 1 inch cubes
1 1/2 cups **water**, for water bath
1/2 cup **raisins**
1 cup **half and half**
1 tablespoon **butter or margarine**, melted
2 large **eggs**
1/4 cup **light brown sugar**
1/4 cup **sugar**
1/2 teaspoon **cinnamon**
1/2 teaspoon **rum extract**
1/8 teaspoon **nutmeg**
whipped cream, to top

5. LET the pressure release naturally for 15 minutes before quick releasing any remaining pressure and safely removing lid. Let cool in the pressure cooker for 10 minutes before attempting to remove the cake or pie pan. Do not attempt to remove the pan while still hot!

6. SERVE warm. To serve: run a knife around the edges of the pudding and then flip upside down onto a serving dish, tapping the bottom until the pudding releases. Top with whipped cream.

 To make a quick and easy rum sauce topping: combine 1 cup sugar, 1/2 cup milk, 1 teaspoon rum extract, 1 tablespoon butter in a sauce pan and sauté on the stove over medium heat. Thicken with 1 tablespoon corn starch mixed into 1 tablespoon water, stirring into sauce while simmering.

DESSERTS

Prep Time	Cook Time			Serves	Temperature
15 MINS	15 MINS			SIX	HIGH

Coconut Custard

DESSERTS

T HIS EXOTIC, YET SIMPLE DESSERT'S COOL flavor and smooth texture goes great after a spicy dinner or just after any dinner… or not even after dinner at all. Basically, I just love custard!

1. SPRAY a metal cake or pie pan (small enough to fit into the pressure cooker with room around the sides) with nonstick cooking spray.

2. ADD water bath water to pressure cooker and place cake or pie pan over top. For best results, place pan on top of a metal pressure cooker rack.

SHOPPING LIST

nonstick cooking spray

1 cup **water**, for water bath

2 large **eggs**

2 large **egg yolks**

1 can **sweetened condensed milk** (14 ounces)

3/4 cup **unsweetened coconut flakes**

1 teaspoon **vanilla extract**

3. MIX remaining ingredients in a mixing bowl until well blended, then pour into the cake or pie pan about 1 1/2 inches high. Depending on the pan size, you may have enough for two batches.

4. COVER cake or pie pan with aluminum foil, securely lock on the pressure cooker's lid and set the cooker to high for 15 minutes.

5. LET the pressure release naturally for 10 minutes before quick releasing any remaining pressure and safely removing lid. Let cool in the pressure cooker for 20 minutes before attempting to remove the cake or pie pan. Do not attempt to remove the pan while still hot!

6. REFRIGERATE for a minimum of 3 hours before serving. To serve: run a knife around the edges of the custard, then flip custard upside down onto a serving dish, tapping the bottom until the custard releases.

Serve topped with fresh mango slices or canned pineapple rings and toasted coconut. Or sauté equal parts dark rum, butter and sugar in a sauce pan for 2-3 minutes for a quick and easy rum sauce!

DESSERTS

PREP TIME	COOK TIME	SERVES	TEMPERATURE
10 MINS	3 MINS	SIX	HIGH

CINNAMON APPLES WITH GRANOLA AND ICE CREAM

DESSERTS

I SHOULD REALLY CALL THIS RECIPE Instant Apple Cobbler; because three minutes simply must be the fastest any cobbler has seen the light of day. It's a tough call as to whether a cobbler is still a cobbler if the topping isn't cooked in the same dish as the fruit, but I'll tell you what, my taste buds certainly can't tell the difference! Steaming hot cinnamo... and ice cold vanilla i... ...erican as Apple CO...

Reduce water to 1 cup

Use flour after cooking to thicken

1. Toss the ... h the flour until they are evenly coated, then place in pressure cooker, cover with remaining cinnamon apple ingredients and stir.

2. SECURELY lock on the pressure cooker's lid, set the cooker to high and cook for 3 minutes.

SHOPPING LIST

Cinnamon Apples

3 red apples, peeled, cored and cut into 3/4 inch slices

1/2 cup **flour**

2 cups **water**

1/2 cup **sugar**

1/4 cup **light brown sugar**

1 tablespoon **butter or margarine**

2 teaspoons **ground cinnamon**

1 teaspoon **vanilla extract**

Topping

8 ounces **granola clusters or granola cereal**

4 scoops **vanilla ice cream**

3. PERFORM a quick release to release the cooker's pressure. Safely remove lid, and let cool for 3 minutes.

4. SPOON the apples into 4 individual serving dishes, top with granola and scoop of vanilla ice cream.

Bob's Tips

To crunch up the granola, try baking it on a sheet pan at 350 degrees until it browns, about 5 minutes. You can also prepare these in advance and keep the individual dishes in the fridge until dessert time, microwaving each on high for 1 minute before topping with the granola and ice cream.

DESSERTS

Key Lime Cheesecake

Desserts

This twist on cheesecake is every bit as refreshing as its inspiration. The tart taste of the key lime wonderfully opposes the sweet and creamy cake without veering too far away from the things you love about a traditional, rich cheesecake.

1. Mix vanilla wafer crumbs with butter and press into the bottom of a 7 inch springform pan to form the crust.

2. Add cream cheese, key lime juice, sugar, eggs, yogurt, flour and vanilla extract to an electric mixer or food processor and mix on medium speed until mixture is well blended and fluffy.

3. Pour the mixture over the crust in the springform pan. Tightly cover the pan with aluminum foil.

4. Pour water into the pressure cooker and place a metal rack on the bottom. Place the springform pan on the rack.

5. Securely lock on the pressure cooker's lid and set the cooker to high for 25 minutes.

6. Let the pressure release naturally for 10 minutes before performing a quick release to release the remaining pressure. Safely remove lid, and let cool in the pressure cooker for 10 minutes before attempting to remove the pan. Do not attempt to remove the pan while still hot!

7. Refrigerate for 1 hour with aluminum foil off (blotting any water on the top of the cake with a paper towel to keep cake dry), then replace aluminum foil and refrigerate an additional minimum of 6 hours before serving topped with whipped cream and fresh lime slices.

Shopping List

1 cup **vanilla wafers**, crumbled

2 tablespoons **butter or margarine**

16 ounces **cream cheese**, softened (2 regular sized bricks)

4 tablespoons **key lime juice**

3/4 cup **sugar**

3 **eggs**

1/2 cup **plain yogurt**

1 tablespoon **flour**

1 teaspoon **vanilla extract**

2 1/2 cups **water**

whipped cream, to top

1 **lime**, sliced, for garnish

Bob's Tips It's an absolute must that real key lime juice be used in this recipe! Real key lime juice has very little color (don't buy anything that's a bright neon green!) and a much more tart flavor than traditional lime juice.

DESSERTS

Prep Time	Cook Time	Serves	Temperature
15 MINS	15 MINS	FOUR	HIGH

Banana Nut Bread Pudding

DESSERTS

HOW THE PRESSURE COOKER BAKES FRESH, warm banana nut bread, then cubes it and turns it into this bread pudding in just 15 minutes I'll never know! Okay, so maybe it isn't doing all that, but this recipe sure tastes like it is!

1. SPRAY a metal cake or pie pan (small enough to fit into the pressure cooker with room around the sides) with nonstick cooking spray and then add bread and pecans to pan.

2. ADD water bath water to pressure cooker and place cake or pie pan over top. For best results, place pan on top of a metal pressure cooker rack.

3. WHISK remaining ingredients except for whipped cream in a mixing bowl until well blended; pour into cake or pie pan over the bread.

SHOPPING LIST

nonstick cooking spray
4 cups **honey wheat sandwich bread**, lightly toasted and cut into 1 inch cubes
1/4 cup **chopped pecans**
1 1/2 cups **water**, for water bath
2 **bananas**, mashed
1 cup **half and half**
1 tablespoon **butter or margarine**, melted
2 large **eggs**
1/4 cup **light brown sugar**
1/4 cup **sugar**
1/2 teaspoon **sugar**
1 teaspoon **vanilla extract**
1/4 teaspoon **cinnamon**
whipped cream, to top

4. COVER cake or pie pan with aluminum foil, securely lock on the pressure cooker's lid and set the cooker to high for 15 minutes.

5. LET the pressure release naturally for 15 minutes before quick releasing any remaining pressure and safely removing lid. Let cool in the pressure cooker for 10 minutes before attempting to remove the cake or pie pan. Do not attempt to remove the pan while still hot!

6. SERVE warm. To serve: run a knife around the edges of the pudding and then flip upside down onto a serving dish, tapping the bottom until the pudding releases. Top with whipped cream.

I like to serve this topped with warm caramel sauce. I've found that making my own caramel sauce from sugar is touchy and troublesome. Store bought sauce is quite adequate and sold in the sundae topping section.

DESSERTS

Prep Time	Cook Time	Serves	Temperature
10 MINS	6 MINS	SIX	HIGH

WHITE CHOCOLATE RICE PUDDING WITH RASPBERRIES

DESSERTS

This rice pudding is unique and delicious without deviating too far away from what you know and love about the standard. It's rich, creamy, full of texture and pleasantly packed with the buttery sweet flavor of white chocolate.

1. PLACE the butter and rice in pressure cooker and stir until rice is coated.

2. COVER with water and securely lock on the pressure cooker's lid. Set the cooker to high and cook for 6 minutes.

3. PERFORM a quick release to release the cooker's pressure. Safely remove lid and stir in remaining ingredients, except for raspberries and garnish.

SHOPPING LIST

1 tablespoon **butter or margarine**, melted

1 cup **Arborio or Calrose rice**

2 cups **water**

1/2 cup **sweetened condensed milk**

1 cup **milk**

1/3 cup **white chocolate chips**

1 teaspoon **vanilla extract**

1/8 teaspoon **nutmeg**

1 pint **raspberries**

shaved white chocolate or additional chips, for garnish

4. LET cool for 10 minutes before stirring again. Serve warm or cover and refrigerate for 2-3 hours and serve chilled. Serve topped with fresh raspberries and shaved white chocolate or white chocolate chips.

I've found that the consistency of rice pudding is a matter of taste. Once chilled, if the pudding over thickens, simply thin it down with more milk until you get it where you like it.

DESSERTS

PREP TIME	COOK TIME		SERVES	TEMPERATURE
15 MINS	15 MINS		SIX	HIGH

CARAMEL CAPPUCCINO FLAN

DESSERTS

This modern twist on the classic Spanish custard dish is an elegant, but simple little pick me up after a great meal. Make the "decaffeinated" version of this recipe by removing the instant coffee and you've got yourself a traditional Caramel Flan.

1. HEAT sugar in a small nonstick pan on the stove over medium heat, stirring occasionally, until a caramel color.

2. SPRAY a metal cake or pie pan (small enough to fit into the pressure cooker with room around the sides) with nonstick cooking spray. Pour caramelized sugar into cake or pie pan and tilt from side to side to coat bottom evenly.

SHOPPING LIST

1/2 cup **sugar**
nonstick cooking spray
1 cup **water**, for water bath
2 **eggs**
1/2 can **sweetened condensed milk** (14 ounces)
1/2 can **evaporated milk** (12 ounces)
2 tablespoons **instant coffee**
1/2 teaspoon **vanilla extract**

3. ADD water bath water to pressure cooker and place sugared cake or pie pan over top. For best results, place pan on top of a metal pressure cooker rack.

4. MIX remaining ingredients in a mixing bowl until well blended, then pour into the cake or pie pan, over top of the sugar about 1 1/2 inches high. Depending on pan size, you may have enough for two batches.

5. COVER cake or pie pan with aluminum foil, securely lock on the pressure cooker's lid and set the cooker to high for 15 minutes.

6. LET the pressure release naturally for 10 minutes before quick releasing any remaining pressure and safely removing lid. Let cool in the pressure cooker for 20 minutes before attempting to remove the cake or pie pan. Do not attempt to remove the pan while still hot!

7. REFRIGERATE for a minimum of 3 hours before serving. To serve: run a knife around the edges of the flan, then flip pan upside down onto a serving dish, tapping the bottom until the flan releases.

If you do not own a cake or pie pan small enough to fit in your pressure cooker, many grocery stores sell disposable pie tins in a full range of sizes. They make cleanup an ease, but are so flimsy that they don't always allow you to remove the flan for serving in one piece!

DESSERTS

Prep Time	Cook Time		Serves	Temperature
15 MINS	25 MINS		SIX	HIGH

PUMPKIN CHEESECAKE

DESSERTS

THE TASTE OF THIS DESSERT'S FALL FLAVORS will bring all the colors of the season to mind. The pumpkin makes the cake slightly smoother than a traditional cheesecake but it's still far more decadent than pumpkin pie with all of its classic flavor!

1. MIX graham cracker crumbs with butter and press into the bottom of a 7 inch springform pan to form the crust.

2. ADD cream cheese, canned pumpkin, sugar, eggs, flour, vanilla extract and pumpkin pie spice to an electric mixer or food processor and mix on medium speed until mixture is well blended and fluffy.

3. POUR the mixture over the crust in the springform pan. Tightly cover the pan with aluminum foil.

SHOPPING LIST

1 cup **graham cracker crumbs**
2 tablespoons **butter or margarine**
16 ounces **cream cheese**, softened (2 regular sized bricks)
1 cup **canned pumpkin**
3/4 cup **sugar**
3 **eggs**
1 tablespoon **flour**
2 teaspoons **vanilla extract**
1 1/2 teaspoons **pumpkin pie spice**
2 1/2 cups **water**
3/4 cup **chopped pecans**, to top
whipped cream, to top

4. POUR water into the pressure cooker and place a metal rack on the bottom. Place the springform pan on the rack.

5. SECURELY lock on the pressure cooker's lid and set the cooker to high for 25 minutes.

6. LET the pressure release naturally for 10 minutes before performing a quick release to release the remaining pressure. Safely remove lid, and let cool in the pressure cooker for 10 minutes before attempting to remove the pan. Do not attempt to remove the pan while still hot!

7. REFRIGERATE for 1 hour with aluminum foil off (blotting any water on the top of the cake with a paper towel to keep cake dry), then replace aluminum foil and refrigerate an additional minimum of 6 hours. Top entire cake with a solid crust-like layer of chopped pecans and dabs of whipped cream before serving.

Unsweetened, canned pumpkin works best in this recipe, not pumpkin pie filling... but pumpkin pie filling would work in a pinch.

Prep Time	Cook Time		Serves	Temperature
15 MINS	15 MINS		FOUR	HIGH

Gingersnap Pear Bread Pudding

Desserts

Gingersnap cookies make this bread pudding anything but day old bread! Add thin sliced pears and you've got a uniquely satisfying combination. I serve it warm, topped with butter pecan ice cream.

1. Spray a metal cake or pie pan (small enough to fit into the pressure cooker with room around the sides) with nonstick cooking spray and then add bread and cookie crumbs to pan. Cover with sliced pears.

2. Add water bath water to pressure cooker and place cake or pie pan over top. For best results, place pan on top of a metal pressure cooker rack.

3. Whisk remaining ingredients except for the whipped cream into a mixing bowl until well blended and then pour into the cake or pie pan over the bread.

Shopping List

nonstick cooking spray
3 cups **French bread**, cut into 1 inch cubes
1 1/2 cups **gingersnap cookies**, crumbled
1 1/2 cups **water**, for water bath
2 **pears**, peeled and sliced 1/6 inch thin
1 cup **half and half**
1 tablespoon **butter or margarine**, melted
2 large **eggs**
1/4 cup **light brown sugar**
1/4 cup **sugar**
1/2 teaspoon **allspice**
1/2 teaspoon **vanilla extract**
1/8 teaspoon **nutmeg**
whipped cream, to top

4. Cover cake or pie pan with aluminum foil, securely lock on the pressure cooker's lid and set the cooker to high for 15 minutes.

5. Let the pressure release naturally for 15 minutes before quick releasing any remaining pressure and safely removing lid. Let cool in the pressure cooker for 10 minutes before attempting to remove the cake or pie pan. Do not attempt to remove the pan while still hot!

6. Serve warm. To serve: run a knife around the edges of the pudding and then flip upside down onto a serving dish, tapping the bottom until the pudding releases. Top with whipped cream.

This recipe is even better when reheated the next day. The flavors have all night to mingle, and mingle they do!

DESSERTS

Prep Time	Cook Time		Serves	Temperature
15 MINS	7 MINS		FOUR	HIGH

Lemon Pudding with Cookie Crumb Swirl

DESSERTS

These days, there's something really fulfilling about making pudding from scratch. You just can't beat the fresh (and tart!) lemon taste of this recipe. Top it with the crumbled vanilla wafer cookies for the perfect presentation.

1. In a mixing bowl, combine all ingredients, except egg whites, water and vanilla wafers.

2. Using an electric mixer, beat egg whites until fluffy enough to leave a slight peak on the end of the beater.

3. Fold the egg whites into the first mixture, and then pour into a cake or pie pan (small enough to fit into the pressure cooker with room around the sides). Cover cake or pie pan with aluminum foil, sealing edges well.

4. Add water bath water to pressure cooker and place cake or pie pan over top. For best results, place pan on top of a metal pressure cooker rack. Securely lock on the pressure cooker's lid, set the cooker to high and cook for 7 minutes.

5. Let the pressure release naturally for 10 minutes before quick releasing any remaining pressure and safely removing lid. Let cool in the pressure cooker for 10 minutes before attempting to remove the cake or pie pan. Do not attempt to remove the pan while still hot!

6. Cover and refrigerate for 2-3 hours before serving. Serve topped with a swirl of vanilla wafer cookie crumbs.

SHOPPING LIST

2 **egg yolks**, beaten
2 tablespoons **flour**
1 tablespoon **butter**
zest of **1 lemon**
2 tablespoons **lemon juice**
1/2 teaspoon **lemon extract**
2/3 cup **milk**
1/2 cup **sugar**
2 **egg whites**
2 cups **water**, for water bath
8 **vanilla wafers**, crumbled

Bob's Tips

The cookie crumb swirl is a wonderful presentation but you may want to keep a handful of whole vanilla wafers on hand to dip into the pudding. Once you get a taste of the crumbs you may want something with a little more substance!

DESSERTS

Recipe Index

Bob Warden

IN THE SEVENTEEN YEARS **BOB WARDEN** has been appearing as a guest cooking expert on **QVC** he has helped develop hundreds of cooking products. With great expertise in pressure cookery, his six models of electronic pressure cookers have been purchased by over 400,000 **QVC** customers. He is also the author of five cookbooks and co-author, along with Gwen McKee, of the *Best of the Best Cook's Essentials Cookbook*. Bob has written *Bob Warden's Slow Food Fast* especially for today's home cook who is looking for quick and easy ways to prepare great, everyday meals, without sacrificing quality or flavor.